The
Excuse Me, Your Life
Is Waiting
Playbook

Revised Edition

LYNN GRAB

DISCARDED

HR

for the evolving human spirit

HAMPTON ROADS
PUBLISHING COMPANY, INC.

Cover and interior design by Maxine Ressler
Cover illustration © Carlos Benigno/iStockphoto.com
Interior illustrations: © Ben Exley, Brett Lamb, and Elena Kalistratova/
    iStockphoto.com; Maxine Ressler; Clipart.com/Jupiterimages
Editor: Addie Johnson Talbott
Production Director: Dennis Fitzgerald
Proofreader: Ashley Benning
Typeset in Bell MT Std and Neutra Text

Hampton Roads Publishing Company, Inc.
Charlottesville, VA 22906
www.hrpub.com

ISBN 978-1-57174-641-2
Library of Congress Cataloging-in-Publication Data available on request

Printed on acid-free paper in Canada
TCP
10 9 8 7 6 5 4 3 2 1

Contents

The *Real* Beginning

Never before, since creation began, has there been such a time as the one in which we are now living.

Never before has so much change been taking place on our planet, so fast.

Never before has there been such a push for mankind to awaken to its true reality, its full potential, its true being-ness.

Never before has this planet had to endure such gargantuan pressures of high frequencies, as are being beamed down to us now.

Never before in recorded science has earth's constant vibration of 7.85 megahertz changed to a frequency of more than double that, as scientists are recording now. And science does not understand.

We are no longer *entering*, we are already *in* the most spectacularly exciting age this little jewel of the universe has ever known, the age for which this planet was designed, and the age that we all came to be a part of.

> Never before, since creation began, has there been such a time as the one in which we are now living.

Mankind is waking up to its own divinity, a process that is both stupendously thrilling and horrifically painful, for the wake-up process demands uncompromising change. Most assuredly, not all share this desire to awaken—much less change—and not all will choose to participate at this time, if ever.

Prophets, seers, and biblical writers have foretold this time for ages. According to their ancient interpretations, sometimes with revelations of apocalyptic horrors, sometimes with visions of the end of time, sometimes with prophecies of rapture beyond imagination, they could see that mankind was in for unimaginable alterations. While these seers were all close, none can claim the brass ring, for what none of those visionary souls could grasp was the whys of these times, or the physics that will—or will not—cause them to become a reality. This is, in part, what you have signed up to help accomplish.

Man (meaning mankind, not the physical being) is in the process of becoming that which it has never been before, a realized god incarnate. Man is becoming a fully aware, fully enlightened, fully awakened Self, a Source (meaning an originator of creation), and a Creator, all in one.

Yet not even the originator of this particular universe knows exactly how it will turn out. All the universes within the omniverse wait and watch with zealous anticipation. "Will it work? Will countless eons of planning and maneuvering pay off? Will mankind birth itself into a new reality and new species of divinity? So far, we're making it. So far, so good. But we're not there, yet!

The call is out, and every single one of us on this planet has gotten that call. This is it. The time is now. It's either you-know-what or get off the pot, which in divine terms translates into "either you get your act together and move into this business of waking up to Who and What you are, or you're going to be left behind—way behind." Why? Because it will be zillions of years before what is being called a "birthing," like the one we're about to experience, will ever happen again. Not a fun thought.

So you picked up a book like this because you are one who feels the push. You are waking up to your own divinity. You sense the urgency to know and to make the connection with your God-self, the God you truly are. You sense the urgency to do whatever needs to be done to allow this never-before-seen event to happen—to you and to all who desire to come on board now. The time is now. This is it. It is time to wake up!

Never, ever alone!

Where did we ever get this foolish idea that we are alone in the universe, or that we're here by some dumb stroke of either good or bad luck?

Where do we come off thinking that divine intervention is exclusive to biblical times, or is just a storyline from a TV show about angels?

> You are waking up to your own divinity.

At this very moment, there are hundreds of thousands of entities in the unseen around the earth, mostly specialists, who are working feverishly to bring about this apex of creation. But we go slobbering about, thinking we're all by our poor lonesomes, that nobody loves us, and that the troubles of the world are on our shoulders alone. No statements ever made could be further from the truth.

We were loved into existence to experience life for that which created us, and to be the extension of that Creator. Once hatched into Light, we took it up from there, learning about rights and wrongs, happiness and pain, and what makes it all happen. Gradually we matured. Then, as physicality became a viable reality, plans were laid for us to become what had never been before—God-man realized. Though such plans were laid countless eons ago, we are now living the execution of that incredible blueprint.

And so, yes, the seers were close. Time *is* collapsing. But there will be no end to our world, although those who *do* believe the end of the world to be close at hand will eventually experience catastrophic horrors. At the same time, a form of Heaven on Earth will be present for many of us, but not for all, for the fear of awakening to one's full, radiant beauty is far too frightening for most, even for those who wait for "the rapture."

Not an easy time

This "birth" will not be all fun and games. With the unfathomably high energies our planet is now receiving to push this process forward, many will crack emotionally under the intensely high pressures. Unresolved issues that may have once been avoidable, or purposely forgotten, will rise like barbaric beasts from within those who insist on denying their divinity. Suicides will be common.

Psychiatrists' couches will be overloaded, as will mental institutions. Deaths of all kinds will increase dramatically through disease, natural disasters, and mechanical failures, such as airplane crashes, as millions upon millions unconsciously choose to remove themselves from the emotional pressures raging around our world today.

One thing you must know: We who decide to accept this challenge to awaken are pioneers of the highest sense. Oh sure, there have been ascensions before, by the thousands. And there have been masters of the esoteric who could teleport and morph and do all those fun things. But no human has been where we are going. No one! *No one has ever become the totality of their own Source.* We are the vanguard, the volunteers who walk in front of the group to slash a path through the untrodden jungle while we get scratched and mauled without thanks for our efforts. (Ah, but someone had to do it!)

One more thing you must know: huge, horrible, mass events such as 9/11 have been *preplanned* by thousands of volunteers (unconsciously) to bring our world back together. The thousands killed in that event were most surely not in negative emotion; they were—and are—saints of the highest order.

Though there are now millions on this path to awakening, most of society remains terrified of us, for we represent a shift so huge, they do not care to even contemplate it. That will not change in our lifetime. You cannot present an entrenched bodily mass—meaning most of mankind—with such a drastic new potential and expect it to welcome the immense changes required with open arms.

What *will* change for us is our way of life. As much of the planet becomes ever more paranoid, *we will awaken one day* to find the exquisite joy of living in a very new world. The good news is we have all the help we require to make this amazing transition. All we have to do is ask, and we will be shown in a wink.

Making way for the new

And that is what this Playbook is all about—cleaning out the old residue to make ready for what's coming down the pike for us, just around the corner.

o It's about reconnecting with old friends in the unseen to help us move through some potentially tough, personal times.

- It's about learning the physics involved in this overnight evolution of the human species.

- It's about taking control of our lives to have the gaiety, prosperity, and ongoing joy that is so necessary to pull off this mind-boggling transition—the creation of divine man.

So crank up your passion and put your fears to rest. Sure, you're going to have some bumps in the road ahead, but who cares? You'll know what to do with them, why they came to you in the first place, and how to turn them into breathtaking rewards.

- You're going to learn the art of deliberate creation instead of creation by so-called happenstance.

- You're going to be getting out of helplessness and into personal control.

- You're going to learn how to take back your divine power to create the fantastic life you have always wanted, while furthering your process of divine metamorphosing at a breakneck speed.

- You're going to learn how to connect with your own divinity, at any time, in any place.

- You're going to learn how to live without pain, or struggle, or even worry.

In short, as you move through this Playbook of Awakening, you are going to learn to become—in a relatively short period of time—the magnificent being you came here to be so that you can move on, go beyond, *and come home* to a newness so unimaginable, books have rarely touched on it. And no book has ever unveiled the step-by-step process of how to get there—until now.

> So crank up your passion
> and put your fears to rest.

How to use this book

Basis for the Twelve Tenets

The basis for the Twelve Tenets of Empowerment comes from two books by Lynn Grabhorn: *Beyond the Twelve Steps: Roadmap to a New Life,* and *Excuse Me, Your Life Is Waiting: The Astonishing Power of Feelings.*

Don't jump ahead

Fun? Absolutely! Intense? Very! So please, do not jump ahead. Take each Tenet as it comes, doing all of the exercises in the order you find them.

If followed as it is laid out, this Playbook will enable you to take complete control of your life, living in joy, abundance, and harmony in a topsy-turvy world on the brink of indescribable change.

For groups or individuals

Whether you are part of a spiritual study group or simply on your own path of enlightenment, this Playbook will rapidly hasten your process of awakening, as well as help you become an expert in the art of creating your world by deliberate intent rather than by chance.

But please note: This is not a textbook. Nor is this a typical self-help book that you sit down to zip through in one reading. The material is far too condensed, and the layout of the pages, far too packed with information and exercises to be read and worked on in any way but slowly, over and over, until the new concepts become a part of you.

For groups

There is no set way for groups to go through this Playbook, but here are a few suggestions:

While at your study group, read through a Principle; then each person can do the next exercise(s) individually while you are all present in the group. Finally, discuss what you found; always discuss what you've found.

Or, read the Principle out loud, discuss it, and then do the next exercise as a group, discussing as you go along, always relating the findings of the exercise(s) back to the information in the Principle.

Or, have each person read the principle and do the exercise(s) at home, bringing them to your study group for an in-depth discussion.

For individuals

As an individual, you may be more challenged to "stay on course" and not jump ahead, skip around, or gloss over areas you find uncomfortable. However, if you will set yourself small, daily—or weekly—goals, such as "I'll read through and complete the exercise(s) on just two pages today, no more, no less," then you will quickly find how easy it will be to ignore the book's imposing size.

But take heart. While the Playbook requires some hefty thinking and strange activities, most of what you're being asked to write is going to be quite new to you, pieces of information very different from anything you've probably ever thought about or have been asked to do or reveal before.

Discuss and/or Journal

For either groups or individuals, "Discuss and/or Journal" sections may require the most profound reflection. As a group, these segments are ideally suited to foster ardent roundtable discussions. As an individual, please journal your thoughts from these questions, for in the writing will come the revelations!

Homework

No, it's not as bad as it sounds. Homework is simply something to be done all the time. In other words, Homework usually pertains to something that will be ongoing, either by writing in a journal, or *feeeeeling* something special, or even looking for things. Actually, the entire Playbook is homework, but these sections ask for specific—and continual—focus.

And finally . . .

You'll see the word "you" printed in two ways: 1) in all lower case letters, or 2) with a capital "Y," as in You.

You'll find the same throughout this book with the word "self," sometimes shown in all lower case letters, and other times with a capital "S."

A capital "Y" in You means the God-you-are You, whereas a small "y" denotes the persona you deem yourself to have or be.

A capital "S" in Self is the same thing, the God-you-are Self, whereas a small "s" is how you view yourself, your persona.

In truth, there may have been times when a capital should have been used or vice versa. Just know that there is a You of you and a Self of yourself who knows all there is to know about you and loves you in spite of it all beyond your wildest comprehension.

And so, let the journey begin. My love goes with you. You are more important than you could ever know.

Tenet One

We realize we are vastly more than our body

WITH THIS TENET WE

o begin the walk out of limitation

o learn where our identity comes from

o open the door to true self-responsibility

o plant the first seeds toward accepting our own divinity

Principle #1 We are thought manifested into a life form

We think we are our bodies; we are not. We think we are our problems, or our ancestors, or our many identities. We are not. We are not our sex, or our illnesses, or our desires. We are not our loves, our pains, or our addictions. What we are is a piece of the All That Is, sired by the light, in order that the "isness" might experience itself greater than it was before.

We are the embodiment of a love so vast, so incomprehensible, that we run from its power. Yet that power is what we are.

We are the higher power that is greater than ourselves.

We are a marvelous creation of mind in matter.

We are the ongoingness and foreverness of everything that is.

We are a portion of the infinite, a piece of God destined to wake up one day and remember just that.

We are incomprehensible forces of energy living for now inside physical instruments, because that is what we chose to do.

We are a portion of the whole; therefore what God is, is what we are.

We are power centers of unlimited magnificence, supreme intelligences who have never been separated from our source, for we are that source.

> We are what we look outside ourselves to find.

We are the love we seek, the joy for which we yearn, the fervor of life we think we have lost. Our longing is but the pressing call of our soul to wake up, and to remember. This, then, is our grand journey home.

2

The Longing Exercise

Understanding what our strange longings have felt like over the years, and how we handled them, helps to clear away any doubts we may have about beginning this journey back to remembrance.

Most of us have felt something was missing in our lives, that there had to be far more to it than a paycheck, a two-car garage, 2.5 kids, and matching towel sets. There was an emptiness we haven't understood and have rarely spoken about, a hollowness we yearned to fill, but never did—or could.

The greatest gift we can give ourselves is to seek to remember who and what we are. The only way we will ever fill that longing is to walk into our own power and accept our divinity while we relish our physicalness.

List some of the ways you've tried to fill that deep longing	Use a word or two to describe how those actions made you feel
Escaping into TV	Useless, down

Discuss and/or Journal

1. What is "thought" to you?
2. Where does it come from?
3. How do we originate it?
4. What does it do? What is its purpose?
5. Can it harm us? Can it help us? How?
6. What does this mean: "We are thought manifested into life-form"?

Do these (1-6) before going on!

What we are is pure, raw, source material manifested into form to learn and understand how to manipulate that energy in physicality. Pure, raw, source material is thought in its highest (frequency) form. Social consciousness is impure source material in one of its lowest (frequency) forms. Either way, we are source material manifested into form.

Who cares anyhow? If we want to stop struggling, we had darn-well better care. If we want to stop pain, we had better care! If we want to create our lives in any way other than what they are right now, we have got to care.

So here's how it comes down: We are not our bodies; we are energy. We are electromagnetic beings, sending out electromagnetic waves that come from our emotions. Every thought we embrace has its own frequency, bringing back to us exactly what we send out. *We are not our body; we are mind IN body.*

> Realize that your present difficulty is only a small part of you, and the rest of you is doing quite well, thank you.

The Blow 'em Up Exercise

Before we can fill that longing and walk into our own divinity, we have to do some dumping.

Jot down anything you can think of in your life today that you'd like to get rid of, dump, or blow up. Emotional pains, economic struggles, family problems, etc. (Leave the past out for now; we'll get to that later.)

1. My job!	6.
2.	7.
3.	8.
4.	9.
5.	10.

Principle #2 We are not our problems

All those things you listed in the previous exercise are just good old-fashioned problems. Until we can at least *entertain* the idea that we are greater than our bodies, we will continue to live for only one thing in life: *our problems!*

We think we are our bodies, and we think we are our problems. Of course, we are neither. Yet holding on to our problems is the very thing that keeps us from filling that longing inside. Once we find our inner core, once we come to know our true Selves, problems vanish. *That's what this Playbook is about!* But before going on, we need to know where our problems come from in the first place!

Discuss and/or Journal

1. What do you think a problem is?
2. Could you describe one of yours in just one sentence?
3. How do you think we get problems?
4. Why do you think we have them?

Please! ⟶
Do these first (1–4)
before going on!

The Emotion Exercise, Part I

First, let's look at the many emotions some of these problems bring up.

Make a list of all the common negative emotions we live with day to day, such as fear, worry, remorse, etc.

The Emotion Exercise, Part II

Deeply and sincerely feel—feeeeel—what it would be like to live without any of those emotions. Share, write, or tell yourself out loud what it felt like without them. Be honest. Was it terrific? Or was it boring and monotonous? Every one of those feelings is a problem! Everything you listed on the previous page is a problem. We are addicted to those feelings. But if they're so uncomfortable, why do we keep them around? It's simple...

> We will never know the greatness of our Selves until we know the source of our pain and struggle, so we are going to look hard at what controls us.

Problems give us our identity!

o Problems are our number one addiction.

☆ We are addicted to negative feelings.

☆ Our lives are a constant acting out of our addictions.

☆ We live for our addiction to our problems, day in and day out.

o Problems give us security.

☆ They are like old friends: known...familiar...predictable.

☆ Problems give meaning to a life without purpose.

☆ To the degree that we deny our true essence, will we have problems.

- Problems and blame go hand in hand.
  - ☆ Because we don't understand how we get what we get, we blame others.
  - ☆ We place blame outside of us for most events in our lives.
  - ☆ The surest way to maintain problems is to maintain blame!

- Problems come from our beliefs.
  - ☆ Beliefs form our reality (as we will come to see).
  - ☆ Beliefs carry powerful emotions.
  - ☆ And emotion is what causes the experience (as we will find out).

Say what? That's right, emotion causes the experience.

The belief creates the problem!

- Every belief we have carries its own emotion.
  - ☆ It's the *emotion* of the belief that's the culprit.
  - ☆ It's the *emotion* behind the belief that magnetically attracts.
  - ☆ A belief is a thought, and thought creates emotion.

- Beliefs make up our subconscious.
  - ☆ Whatever we believe, we live.
  - ☆ Whatever we believe, we attract.
  - ☆ Or...whatever we believe, we repel.

- Beliefs create our reality.
  - ☆ If we believe a thing, the effect will follow, no matter what.
  - ☆ If we believe a thing, we will experience what we believe.
  - ☆ Until we can control our beliefs, they will control us.

Belief

Belief Exercise, Part I

Everything we're doing on these next four pages has to do with beliefs. Fear, blame, "if-onlys": they are all powerful beliefs we hold that continue to form our experience day after day. Take blame. Because we don't understand why we can't get what we want, we usually blame others for our not having it. That's a belief.

Putting down what you think you "should" write will accomplish nothing. There is no right or wrong here, but your deeply truthful response will be your most important step toward realizing how far we all go to maintain our powerlessness. You will refer to these exercises often, so please, dig down! NOTE: Do the left column BEFORE filling in the other two: then go back and quickly fill in the two right columns.

Do this column first!

Some of the things I fear are . . .	Quickly jot down who's to blame	Why are they responsible?
Being fired	My boss	He has control

Belief

Belief Exercise, Part II

By placing blame outside of ourselves we give up choice, we look to others to make us feel better, we give up control, and we give our power away.

We all have a pocketful of "if-onlys": "If only I had…," "If only I could…," "If only I hadn't…," "If only they had…," "If only it would…," "If only we could…," "If only she/he/it had…," "If only we were…," "If only they would…." Blame is just another form of belief. As we change our beliefs, we change our experience. Try not to skimp on this; we can't change our lives until we change our beliefs.

List your "if-onlys" "If only I…"	Who's to blame for it	Why are they responsible?
Were smarter	My folks	Their folks?

Okay, this is a start. Do we have to cough up every fear, all of our blames, every "if-only," and every long-forgotten belief that we've buried somewhere? Absolutely not! We just need to be aware we've had a lot of beliefs that have been raising holy hell with us, causing our lives to be a long way from all we had hoped.

Explanation Break

"If this Tenet is about us being more than our bodies, how come we're into all this stuff about beliefs, beliefs, beliefs?"

Here's how come: We touched on it lightly, but now let's really look at it. If we can swallow the notion that our beliefs create our experience, that our entire physical environment is the materialization of our beliefs, that our beliefs form every moment of our reality, and that if we really believe a thing, the effect will follow whether we want it to or not… well, if we can ultimately swallow all that, we just might realize how unimaginably powerful we are.

Sure, a lot—if not most—of our beliefs have come from others, but until we can see that we are not at their mercy unless we believe we are, we remain in that vicious circle where we're constantly reinforcing all the stuff we're trying so desperately to change. And wondering why it's not happening!

Here's the bottom line: Until we can completely and unequivocally accept the idea that our beliefs form our reality, our reality is not going to change. Period! And we will never, but never, come to believe that we are any greater than these dear bodies. Yes, the bodies are a wonder, but they are simply not what we are. Never have been, never will be. So if we can match up at least some of our beliefs with some of our problems, and vice versa, we just might be willing to accept that we are ever so much more than our bodies.

Two kinds of beliefs

Universal: These are the beliefs common to many, such as "humans will always kill," or "you have to work hard to get ahead." These are the ones we build our lives from. Because they are so common, they are also powerful, making them a major influence in our daily affairs.

Personal: Yours alone, such as "I'm too fat," or "I'm not handsome."

It doesn't matter a hoot how many of each kind of belief you list in these next two exercises, only that you are aware of how much the beliefs of others—that you have adopted as your own—control your life. Do everything you can to connect a belief to a life experience. Perhaps a belief is "Short men are rotten lovers." Or "Women aren't as smart as men." Or "I'll never get ahead financially." Any kind of habitual thoughts you have that are limiting. Ready? Go for it.

Belief Exercise, Part III-a

Everything you listed in Part I and II is a problem that came from a belief. And every negative belief you hold causes some kind of problem. This exercise will clearly show how we run our lives—so unnecessarily—from our beliefs.

This is one of the most important exercises in this Playbook. Please! Take time, feel it through, go way back, be honest. This could be a long list, so use extra pages in your notebook, if necessary.

This side first!
↓

List your BELIEFS	List the PROBLEMS they cause
I'm short on education	Limits me getting ahead

continued . . .

List your BELIEFS	List the PROBLEMS they cause

When you finally understand that you can generate that which you have been desperately looking for outside of yourself, you become the master of your life.

Belief

Belief Exercise Part III-b

Now we turn it around. Please note that these pages have not been put side by side, facing each other. That's for a very good reason. Start as fresh as you can with a new problem, one not listed on the other page. This will conjure up a fresh belief. You might not be able to finish these two exercises in one day (III–a and b), but keep adding to the list as you think of more throughout the days.

This side first!
↓

List your PROBLEMS	List the BELIEFS they cause
My car's a wreck	My car's a wreck

HOMEWORK: *Belief Busting*

How do we get rid of those beliefs we now see as destructive? One way is to play "let's pretend" to generate the emotion *opposite* the one that comes from the belief you want to change.

One-a-day

The more often you generate that new feeling, the faster you'll change what you want to change. Every day pick a belief you hold about yourself (whether universal or personal) and conjure up the opposite *feeeeeling*. One-a-day! For instance, let's say you believe yourself to be a people-pleaser. So you conjure up the *feeeeeling* of saying "No," or walking away, or letting someone get their *own* coffee. If you believe yourself to be shy, conjure up the *feeeeeling* of being gregarious, interested in people, a good conversationalist, etc. Pretend. Ask your guidance for help, and then STAY ALERT for the miracles that will begin to happen.

> Stay alert for the miracles that will begin to happen.

One-a-week

If you've got a real stickler, work on it for a whole week. Play. Have fun. Conjure up new images that bring up new feelings. As you'll soon see, *feeeeelings* are what make this all happen, because as you feel, you become. The more you do this homework, you will literally create a new internal blueprint from the neuro-pathways that are being imprinted in your brain. But you must get into it emotionally, or it will just be a waste of time. If you don't *feeeeel* it, forget it!

Now be physical

When you're ready, take this to the next level and *physically* act out the opposite of what you want to change. You're still pretending, but now you are energy in motion, creating new pathways for your brain to respond to.

For instance ... shy? Then smile at someone. Believe you are poor? Then put a fifty-dollar bill in your wallet. Believe you are a timid speaker? Then get in front of your mirror and cut loose.

Imagination is the closest we get to divinity in physicality. So imagine! Be sure to always generate the new emotion that is opposite the old one. Do this regularly, and you will soon find yourself becoming a deliberate—rather than accidental—creator of your experience. And always, always, make this fun!

> Change the feeling, and you'll change the belief.

Principle #3   What we see in the mirror is only an instrument

For ease of reference now, we're going to call that vaster portion of ourselves our "entity." It is the unlimited and indefinable being we truly are, reaching far beyond our limited ideas of God. So, if this vast something is what we really are, what is it we see when we look in the mirror?

Deep inside each of us is a little spark that is incomprehensibly powerful. That little spark is what we are, for it is a piece of our entity. It is All That Is, learning to experience more of itself in this wondrous thing called a body. Inside us, our entity can explore its potential and understand more of what it is, meaning more of what *we* are.

However, let's not downplay the body. While it is no-where near the totality of what we are, it holds the knowl-edge of all that has ever been or ever existed anywhere in any universe. Our journey, then, is to get the two together, entity and body. This is the journey home, the journey into remembrance, the journey back to the love from which we came and from which we were made. This is the creation of heaven on earth.

As soon as we allow ourselves to explore possibilities be-yond physicality, our minds will open like whirlwinds. No, we're not talking "spirit world" omnipresence. And no, we don't get there by dying, for dying is just stepping into an-other frequency that feels good, but where we're still basi-cally physical. What we're talking about here is learning to touch the realness of ourselves *while still in this body*. When we can reach in and touch that life spark, we step into a world of incomprehensible joy. We've mastered physicality, and we'll never have to do anything else except play out our physical games for the remainder of time we choose to stick around.

If you have this book, you're hell-bent on discovering who you really are, because you've heard the call of the entity-you. You're working to find yourself, to understand yourself. Above all (and with the relieved assistance of your delighted entity), you're working to slice away at that thing we call "image" so you can touch the true You that lies within.

Image! That's the operative word here. Until we can see that image has been dictating our lives, not much is going to change. So we're going to work at slicing away at that image, forcing new joy and new feelings into these bodies. We'll have a sharp awareness of what our images are doing. And we're going to work toward eliminating our boundar-ies, one by one, until there will be nothing for us to do but live from that inner spark, in joy, in harmony with all Life.

The God Exercise

Before we can aim at where we're going, we need to know where we've been.

On the left, list some ideas of how you used to (or still do) think about God. On the right, note where you believe those ideas came from: family, church, friends, etc.

I used to think that God . . .	Those ideas probably came from . . .

Discuss and/or Journal

1. I *now* believe that God is . . .
2. Can you handle being a divine presence? If so, explain how it feels.
3. What do you think is the biggest block to believing in your divinity?

Do these first before going on!

You are a child of the stars, sired by the light. Wake up to what you really are and always have been. You are the same energy as the universe, the pure positive energy of All That Is. Your will and God's are one and the same; only your ego tells you differently. See if you can repeat the following statements without flinching. If you can't, leave them alone for a few weeks, then come back to them later.

Say them over and over. Make yourself *feeeeel* what you are saying, even if it terrifies you. If you can, allow yourself to feel the love, the beauty, the preciousness, the awesomeness, and the *truth* of what you speak.

God's will and mine are the same.

I am not good; I am not bad. I am all that is, meaning all the good and all the bad.

There is not now, nor has there ever been, any person or power greater than that which I am.

I am the pure, positive, ever-flowing, ongoing energy of the universe.

I am a pinch-off of the source; therefore, the source and I are one.

I cannot separate myself from the energy from which I came.

I am a being of love and light, more powerful than 10,000 suns.

I can become whatever I desire to be.

I am forever.

I am not my body, my ego, or my problems.

I am what I have always been . . . I have only been wearing a mask.

Feeling the God you are

Get yourself centered . . . ask those who walk with you for assistance . . . ask your inner being, your life spark, for assistance . . . and now express your desire to feel your God-energy, for indeed, it is what you are. It is not apart from you now, nor has it ever been.

Go inside to that safe place where your life spark resides, that place just behind your heart . . . open up to your inner being . . . allow the feeling of love to wrap you . . . it is an energy vortex that will come if you will express your desire to feel it. So express, ask, invite.

Focus on the heart area, and now bathe yourself in love. Wrap yourself in a blanket of loving warmth. Yes, do it yourself . . . *to* yourself, then stay alert for whatever may happen within your body.

> **INSIGHT**
> The more we become aware of who and what we truly are, the fewer problems we have.

Now repeat to yourself, "I am love, I am love, I am love." Then change it to "I am loved, I am loved, I am loved." Keep your focus on your heart area. "I am loved . . . I am loved . . . I am loved . . . I am loved."

Over and over and over, in the stillness of your being, in the quiet of your person, ask again and again to feel the love.

You may feel heat . . . you may feel a wash of love . . . you may have tears . . . you may feel nothing. There is no right or wrong. If you felt nothing, not to worry. You will. For what God is, you are.

You need only ask to connect with your entity, and one day . . . one wonderful day, you will feel that brief moment of indescribable love flood over you. Look for it. Ask for it. It is you.

Tenet Two

We accept that we are not separate, not alone; we are one with All That Is

WITH THIS TENET WE

o begin to fill the emptiness within

o are introduced to frequencies of thought

o begin the move out of social consciousness

o start the not-so-long journey back to oneness

Principle #1   Separation is an illusion

Since long before Jesus ever walked the face of this earth, man has felt himself as apart from his "maker." When the words of what would become the Bible were finally put into print, they not only continued to foster the erroneous belief that man was separate from his maker, but served to cement that belief. Though the words of Jesus echoed over and over that "the Father and I are one," there was enough misinterpretation of his work imbedded within the biblical pages to secure the impenetrable belief that man was a lowly, sinful creature to be punished righteously by a vengeful being from the unseen.

'Tain't so! The aborigines know it. The Native Americans and a bunch of others know it. It's all the rest of the world that feels alone, abandoned, rejected, and … *separate.*

Every one of us was loved into existence for the express purpose of exploration, expansion. The source from which we came wanted to know itself better. It wanted to know its capabilities, its weaknesses, its greatness. So it created different "faces" of itself in order to know itself better. Each of us is one of those different faces, pinched off from our source with the full intent that we would always be equal to it.

And we are. However, from the instant we were pinched off, so to speak, we began to feel some separation. And why not?! We had been one, total consciousness, then all of a sudden we're just a piece on our own, not part of the whole. And moving into that new medium called "time and space" didn't help any, either. Now we really felt abandoned. But more than that, we felt confused.

Over the countless eons, that feeling has never left. More times than not, we've felt downright hostile, as an abandoned kid might feel toward his parents. Yet, deep within, we've maintained an elusive remembrance that we were perhaps a part of something much grander than our own selves.

It was that very feeling, that unspoken, unlooked-at gnawing that gave birth to the "me here, God out there" syndrome. We no longer held the total knowingness of the whole, so what were we? We knew we were separate packages of something, but of what? And in that separation, we started hurting and feeling isolated and very, very alone.

But now that deep feeling of aloneness, and our frustration of not knowing who we truly are, is pushing us to wake up and remember, a push that is coming directly from our soul, the divine record-keeper of our being. Our soul has acquired all the feelings and experiences of separation that it can handle and is doing everything possible to force us into remembrance of where we came from and who we are, so that it can get on with what it was created to do in the first place—record the joys and experiences of being one of the faces of the whole.

Why has this taken so long? Why hasn't this awful feeling (that none of us ever talk about) been dealt with before—like eons ago? Because our fear and pain were so great, and created such a block, we could never hear our source calling to us, saying, "Hey, come on! We're all one. You are not separate from me, and I am not separate from you. We're the same thing. Hello! Hello! Hello! Did you hear me??? *We are the same being.*"

> Like the leaves of a tree, we are individualized pieces of the whole.

And so now, with the soul saying it can no longer operate in this environment of forgetfulness, that life within us— our true divinity—is beginning to wake up. It's beginning to hear through our doubts, and our fears, and our isolation. It's beginning to respond to the soul's incessant pushing. That life spark within us wants dearly to awaken. It wants to remember where it came from so that, for the first time in its physical existence, it can enjoy its true reality as an *individualized portion* of the whole: God, in a body.

The push of the soul is happening to everyone all over our planet, yet only a few are far enough out of their anxieties of aloneness to hear the call. You have heard. And so now this book comes to you, compliments of your frustrated soul and awakening life spark. You are on your road to remembrance, on your road to awakening, called *home.*

The Aloneness Exercise

Once again, until we know where we've been, it's impossible to take deliberate aim at where we're going.

Reach down into your depths to find the times you felt deeply alone. Maybe it was after a breakup, maybe feeling new to a setting such as school or a job. Maybe it was just driving in the car. Maybe it's now. No matter how painful, pull those moments back. They are the prerequisite to remembering You. Note the event, then describe your feelings at the time.

1.

2.

3.

4.

5.

6.

Discuss and/or Journal

As long as we maintain that there is a power greater than ourselves, outside of ourselves, apart from ourselves, we remain in separation, struggle, pain, and hurt.

1. Did you only list a few "aloneness" events? If so, why? There is not one among us who has not felt lonely, abandoned, rejected, separated, isolated, or in some way apart *from*, and felt it thousands of times. Call to those who walk with you for help and support, then go back and finish the list! Denial keeps us in ego, never in God-self.

2. Think back to several of those times, and describe how close to—or separate from—your God you felt at that time.

3a. Take one of those items you listed on the previous page and get back into feeling the unpleasant feelings you described relative to the event.

3b. Now, while trying to hold on to that unhappiness, pretend that you *know* you are the creator, the source, the infinite intelligence of all that is, the oneness. Get into that knowing. You are omnipotent.

3c. While you are being all-knowing, all-powerful, and totally ecstatic, can you still feel those various hurts or pains from the previous page?

4. Stay in the feeling of divine omnipotence and try to pull back the hurt or pain of one or two of your other "aloneness" events.

a. Did the event feel different?
b. Did you feel different *in* the event?
c. Could you get to the feeling-point with any of the events where they simply lost all importance?
d. Write down anything else you felt that was different, or not normal, being sure to cover each event. Be explicit!

> The single greatest cause of emotional pain on this planet is separation. As we accept our oneness, pain vanishes.

If you are in a group, with gentleness, kindness, and above all else, understanding, compare notes. How many did each of you list? See if you can find out, ever so gently, why someone finished only a few items. Where is the resistance? What are they afraid of feeling? (Or was it you?) Then ask the same questions of everyone, "4a" through "4d." Discuss, discuss, discuss.

Have all the possible scenarios of separation been mentioned? Have someone make a list of all feelings that have been mentioned or written down, then find more.

Principle #2 — There is no such thing as a victim, only those who choose to play victim roles

"Oh, sure. Easy for you to say. So tell me—if there are no victims, how come I was abused as a kid?"

The more civilized man became,
  the more separate he felt.
The more separate he felt,
  the more fearful he became.
The more fearful be became,
  the more alone he felt.
The more alone he felt,
  the more he struggled.
The more he struggled,
  the more he blamed.
The more he blamed,
  the more he lived life as a victim.

We're going to leave the actual physics of living as a victim to later Tenets, but for now, we need first to see the confinement in which a victim lives, and to thoroughly understand that, in fact, a victim has no life at all, and never will have.

The Really Serious Victim Exercise

The short list: Memorable—really memorable—happenings

Wherever you feel you have been victimized in your life, either now or in the past, jot it down in three or four words; e.g., "Billy broke my arm," "Boss fired me," "Mountain fell on me." We've all been living as victims, so please don't hold back to be politically correct. If you feel you were a victim, PUT IT DOWN!!!

Victims are not born; they are made.

Victim

Discuss and/or Journal, then Scribble.

Here, in the triangulation of life, is the basis of what we are, either Victim or Master. **First:** *Discuss the words written on the corners and center. How does "Persecutor" or "Rescuer" fit into being a victim? What about "Fear"? What does "Sleeping God" mean?* **Second:** *After you have explored the three points, write at least fifty more words all over the page and all over the triad, as a continuation of the samples below; words that pertain to being a victim. There are hundreds of such words. If you can't find at least fifty, watch some soap operas.*

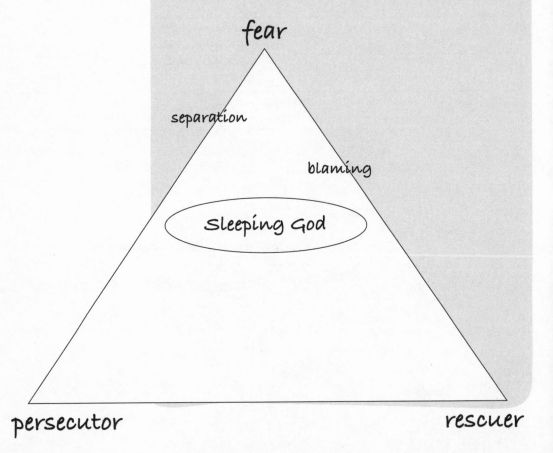

fear

separation

blaming

Sleeping God

persecutor

rescuer

Master

Do the same thing here. True, we haven't discussed "mastery," but you already know what that is. Deep in your own knowingness, you know. You know you are not separate, you know you are not alone, you know you are a master of your destiny and daily life. You know. You already know, and always have.

We have been living a game, pretending we've forgotten, pretending we are at the mercy of life's quirks, pretending we can't help it. But under it all, there's that little voice that says, "Ah, c'mon. Wake up. You created it all for the experiences. You're not a victim, you're a master incarnate. Own up to it."

What is a master? What do the corner and center words mean? Discuss, then write at least 50 words that match your concept of "master."

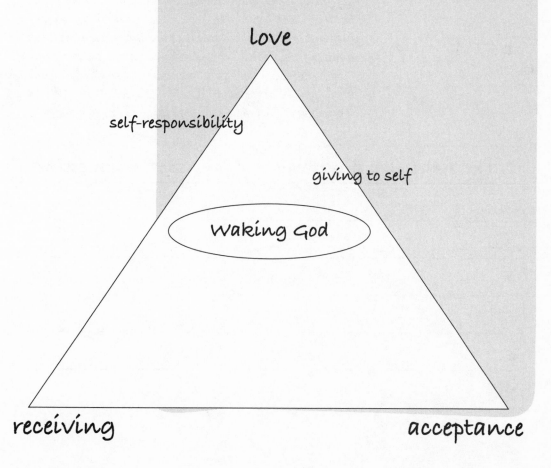

love

self-responsibility

giving to self

Waking God

receiving

acceptance

The "Hell, it happens every day" Victim Exercise

The bigger list: Everyday events

As long as we see ourselves as victims of circumstance, we will never gain the emotional experience of the event, and shall repeat it in some way or other over and over and over.

Now that you've explored many more aspects of victimhood, it's time to put aside guilt and shame at how much you may have participated in this game since birth (like all of us), and get into the nitty-gritty of your life as a victim.

Again, we're not trying to understand here how it all happened; we're only interested right now in seeing how much we've all lived believing we had to live at the mercy of happenstance, without choice. List the littlest things you can think of, like, "Waitress spilled wine on me; stained suit," "Rear-ended; couldn't go to ball game," "Pulled too many dandelions; strained back." DON'T HOLD BACK!!! List a minimum of ten now, then keep this ongoing.

1. The dorky cab driver was lost; I missed my meeting.

2.

3.

4.

5.

6.

7.

8.

9.

10.

Keep this list going!!
The more you find to list
the faster you'll "get it!"

A Quick Rundown on How Victims Play the Game

Remember: someone who feels separated will always think of themselves as a victim.

The World of Victims

Victims . . .
- ❏ live in powerlessness
- ❏ take little responsibility for their feelings
- ❏ are joyless, because they have given away their power
- ❏ are not the boss of their lives; rather *everything* and *everyone* else is
- ❏ play into dramas, and . . .
- ❏ judge the players relentlessly
- ❏ feel like helpless pawns being moved around
- ❏ need to stay in pain; it is their primary addiction
- ❏ think they are forged from without
- ❏ base their lives on "uncontrollable circumstances"
- ❏ think that all of life's circumstances have been unrequested
- ❏ always blame (especially God)
- ❏ live in the past, and so cannot create their desired future
- ❏ feel very comfortable in their role, because they chose it
- ❏ live by "shoulds"

Check off the ones that most pertain to you. Then, can you add nine more?
(Oh come on . . . there are hundreds more!)

Since we draw to us what we *feeeeel*, victims continue to perpetuate their sense of powerlessness.

And How a Master Doesn't Play at All

Those going for their Master's are going for empowerment, back to remembering, out of separation, and out of aloneness

The World of Masters-in-Training

Masters . . .

- ❑ choose what is desired, for the joy of it
- ❑ allow, without judgment
- ❑ are always in control
- ❑ are in the flow of life
- ❑ act, whereas victims always RE-act
- ❑ are owned by no one, no place, no thing
- ❑ know they create it all, minute to minute, decade to decade
- ❑ understand maneuvers, because they have maneuvered
- ❑ choose calm where there is chaos
- ❑ no longer play into dramas; they ignore them
- ❑ no longer give themselves away to the world
- ❑ blame no one or no thing—for anything
- ❑ always move on without regret, *no matter what*
- ❑ never cop out to "God's will" or "fate" or "luck" (either good or bad)
- ❑ know their divinity, and work daily to magnify that feeling

Check off the ones that most pertain to you. Surely you can add more.
(Of course you can)

Stepping out of victimhood is like coming home after a long absence, and being introduced to yourself for the first time.

"Alright already! So how do we go for our Master's?"

By raising our frequencies. That's how.

Everything we do from here on in will be about raising our frequencies so that we will never again feel alone or separated. Instead, we will feel at one with the world, sure of ourselves, in control of our lives, at peace instead of in pieces, creative, abundant. Oh, and happy!

Raising frequencies means stepping out of social consciousness. It means we no longer allow vibrations of negative thinking to control us. It means we will be trading fear-based vibrations for those of joy, sureness, safety, and abundance.

Only by raising our frequencies out of negative feelings can we move into empowerment. And that means we can no longer think like everyone else, or react like everyone else, or feel like everyone else. It means we have to have the courage to change. And that's what all the rest of this Playbook is about: changing from victim to master by deliberately raising our frequencies from fear-based to as close as we can come to joy-based.

Going for our Master's means we give up games, we stop blaming the world for our troubles, we learn to approve of everything we have ever done in order to live a life without one single regret. It means that during the day, we'll have to watch what we say and think, for that causes us to feel, which creates the frequency vibrations that cause us to attract.

Going for our Master's means our whole body will begin to change frequencies as we move closer and closer to our expanded selves. We will actually begin attracting our desires from those higher vibrations with incredible speed.

Our absolute birthright is to create a life that will make us happy, that will bring us all that we have ever desired, when and where we desire it to be. Becoming a Master is learning to flip the switch between frequencies. As we learn to do this (and it doesn't take long at all), we begin the rapid walk up our spiritual mountain to the inexplicable freedom—*in a body*—we came here to experience.

Principle #3   We are never, ever alone

First of all, you can't even get into this place we call Earth without at least two old buddies in the unseen to walk with you daily. Usually they're old friends from other times and lives, or other realities. But whoever they are, they are always, always with you. Always! But even more important is the unfathomable love in which we are held, so unconditional, so intense, so utterly absolute.

"If I'm so loved, how come I can't feel it?"

Ah, there's the rub. It's called self-worth, something we have to give to ourselves before we can, first, accept and, second, feel that incredible force of love. The universe (meaning the All That Is that pinched us off into existence) is the most loving, beautiful thing we could ever find, and we push it away. All it wants to do is to nurture us, hold us, envelope us in its love. But for us to feel that love, we would have to acknowledge our power. And to acknowledge our power, we would have to feel worthy to do so.

So here are the facts:

o We have no idea how great is the strength we carry within us, the power of the infinite.

o That power walks with us every moment of every day.

o We have many friends in the unseen walking with us.

o We are loved far beyond our meager understanding of the word, for we have never been anything but a grand god-in-a-bod trying desperately to understand who and what it is.

- We cannot be here alone.
- From the energy that birthed us (that we are), to our entity (our expanded self), to our buddies who guide us daily, we are never, ever alone.

HOMEWORK: *6 Steps to Feeling Loved*

1. Find a special place where you can go alone, preferably outside, or else somewhere that can be your secret, special place.
2. Spend 15 minutes there each day for 30 days.
3. Make yourself very, very comfortable, always in the exact same place.
4. Think ONLY about you, your value as a human being, your right to be, your right to be loved.
5. Do not let in so much as one tiny problem; they must stay behind.
6. Ask those who walk with you to surround you with their love.

This is guaranteed to work if you'll allow the feelings to come.

Unconditional love does not mean loving in spite of conditions. It means recognizing that loving is the only condition!

Feeling the love you are

Go to that safe, secure place within, and become still. Once you are centered into your being, call . . . in your own words . . . for all of the following entities to join you and to assist you in this meditation.

Call for your guides.

Call for more of your expanded self, your entity.

Call for your favorite archangel.

Call for Pan, the diva of all nature spirits.

Call for the diva of healing.

Call for those who have been or are now your spiritual teachers.

Call for any saints to whom you feel close.

> **INSIGHT**
> When we know who walks beside us on our chosen path, fear becomes impossible.

Now ask that one from each group, one at a time, come up to you and embrace you for at least a full minute. As that is happening, extend your love back to the entity who is embracing you. Let it overflow from you to that entity until you can feel no difference . . . until you cannot tell if it is you loving, or if it is you being loved.

When the first group has embraced you, ask that another guide, another spiritual teacher (they will usually be highly evolved masters), and another of your favorite saints (if you called for more than one) come up to you and touch you first on the right shoulder, and then on the left. Give yourself permission to feel the experience.

And now put yourself in the middle of a hugging circle, and ask that all who are present form about you in one large, very divine hug. Allow your feelings, your tears. When you are ready, thank all who came. Ask that they help you to be aware of their love during the day.

When you are flowing out the energy
of love, you are loving yourself.

Tenet Three

We understand that all circumstances are our own creation

WITH THIS TENET WE

o **pave the way to become deliberate creators**

o **see how all—*all*—creation comes from feeling**

o **find we operate in a sea of electromagnetic energy**

o **see that nothing is created by accident, luck, or happenstance**

Principle #1   We are electromagnetic beings

Everything that is … is energy. You … me … a leaf … the table … a lake … a rubber band. And on this planet, as on many others, energy is electromagnetic. That makes you, me, your in-laws, your car, and your boss all electromagnetic time bombs.

Since we're nothing but electromagnetic energy, we're basically magnets—hugely powerful, highly charged magnets walking around in an energy fog, not having the faintest idea that every moment of every day we're magnetizing into our world every single thing that happens to us, good or bad.

How? It's so simple, it's embarrassing. Yet we've never known this before. Here's what all the positive thinking books missed (came close to, but missed). Here is what governs how our world runs. Here is why there's no such thing as a victim. Here's what will change your life in whatever way you want it changed. Here is the power we were given at birth, that no one ever taught us, because no one ever knew. (Actually, we've always known this, but we forget it all the minute we pop in here.)

All life, all happenings, all circumstances, all luck is based on one simple principle of physics: **"Like frequencies (vibrations) attract."**

Everything we get in life—or don't get—is based on that principle. Every car accident, every lottery win, every death, rape, wedding, raise, or divorce is based on that principle. We are electromagnetic beings. What comes or doesn't come to us does so because we, and we alone, have caused it.

Here are the actual mechanics of how we attract or repel absolutely every event in our lives.

1. Everything that is … is energy, including us.
2. All energy vibrates; therefore, so do we.
3. "Like" vibrations attract "like" vibrations.

> Ready for some good luck? Then check how you're feeling, because the way you think causes the way you feel, and the way you feel causes how you vibrate, and how you vibrate IS the luck you make!

4. The way we think causes the way we feel.

5. Every feeling has its own vibration.

6. Therefore, we attract only by the way we *feeeeeel*.

It's our *feelings* (emotions) that make things happen, not our thoughts. True, our thoughts cause different *feelings*, but just thinking a thought, or visualizing, won't do a thing. It's the *feeling* created from the thought or visualization that creates (as well as the *feelings* we generate *without* thought).

Our *feelings* are pure magnetic energy. They're flowing out from us every moment of every day as a vibrational frequency. This means that HOW we've been *feeling* will affect what kind of magnetic vibration we're sending out.

You could say we're like musical instruments. Sometimes we have lovely high notes and are sending out high-frequency vibrations. Those are always positive feelings—and very magnetic. Other times, in fact most of the time, we're sending out low-frequency, negative vibrations. All those "common emotions" you listed on page 4 in Tenet One are all low-frequency, negative feelings, meaning when you're having them, you're transmitting negatively, therefore *attracting* negatively. Why? Because like vibrations attract their match. Ping a tuning fork in Yankee Stadium that's filled with 10,000 other tuning forks, and only the ones that are calibrated exactly like yours will ping back. No others. Like vibrations attract like vibrations.

High, Fast Vibrations are the feel-good kind of stuff. And they feel good because they are closer to what we are. These are divinely generated *feelings*.

Low, Slow Vibrations are all fear-based social consciousness kind of stuff. These are physically generated feelings. The horror is that unless we're on some kind of downer, or really into a fear or worry that doesn't feel good, all low, slow vibrations seem perfectly natural to us. Here's how it works. Frighteningly simple.

The way we think … causes the way we feel …

… and the way we feel … causes the way we vibrate …

… and the way we vibrate … IS HOW WE ATTRACT!!!

-/+ The Negative/Positive Word Exercise

Negative feelings or emotions are totally foreign to the body, which is why they don't feel good. Negative feelings begin with the negative thought ... which creates the feeling ... which generates the low vibrational frequency that shoots through the body as an electrical charge, then leaves in magnetic waves. Positive feelings are always of a higher frequency, and are far more in tune with the body and closer to what we are, which is why they feel so good.

List all the negative feelings you can possibly think of. Be sure not to leave out all the common little ones like worry, concern, annoyance, etc. Then, listing positive feelings may be more difficult, so feel free to check your dictionary.

Don't pass up this kindergarten exercise; it's the foundation of this whole book!

Negative Feelings	Positive Feelings

Discuss and/or Journal

1. Which side on the previous page had more listings, and why?
2. Did you have a hard time thinking up positive feelings? Explain why.

Do first, before moving on

3. Did you resist or pooh-pooh listing the littlest kind of negative emotion? If so, what do you think your resistance was?
4. Were you able to fill the entire left column? If not, explain why not.

Open a dictionary to any page and notice how many words on that page depict negative emotions. Negative words are the pillars of our language. While you're there, look for positive words. What did you find? What do you make of it?

 ## HOMEWORK: *Our Negative World*

During your day, while listening to the radio or TV, or coworkers, or your children or spouse or friends, or people standing in line at the market, tune in to their habit of negativity. Look for:

1. How often people speak negative words or sentences
2. How normal "negative" is, how common, how much a part of life
3. How often people respond negatively to a positive statement
4. How their faces look, regularly
5. How their body language matches their speaking
6. How they have to have problems to discuss
7. How they cannot accept praise
8. How useless everything seems to them
9. How victimized they feel
10. How helpless they feel

The Most Important Exercise in This Book

As soon as you can truly identify the difference in frequency between a negative and a positive feeling, you can learn to flip from the low negative frequency to high, no matter what is happening around you.

Pick one negative feeling from your Negative/Positive Feelings List, and one positive (no more, to start with). Put the negative one in the left column below, and the positive one in the right. Now FEEEEEL that negative emotion. Get into it. Let yourself go. (Don't worry about your magnetism, you'll balance out in a moment.) If it's hate, go for it! If it's disgust, get into it! Notice how your body feels. (Normal, right?)

Now ... "flip-switch" (instantly change over) to the positive feeling you wrote down (it does not have to be the exact opposite from your negative feeling—any positive feeling will do). Do it instantly, from the negative feeling to whatever positive feeling you put in the positive column. Stay with this one for a longer time until you can feel it wrap you in its embrace of high vibrations. You are now in God-energy! Notice how good it feels.

Notice if you sense a subtle tingling in your body. Notice if you can pump it up even more. Try to do that. Notice how good you feel while you bathe in the high vibrations flowing through you and from you. You are now flowing the pure positive energy of All That Is ... or You! Do the same with your next set of negative/positive words, and your next, until you become completely aware of the difference in physical feeling between negative and positive.

continued . . .

Feel-Bads	Feel-Goods
guilt	excitement

 ## Discuss and/or Journal

1. What did you experience?
2. Could you feel the difference between the two? Explain.
3. Did you notice a very subtle tingling in your body? Explain.
4. Did you find it easier to get into positive energy as you went along?
5. Which negative one was easiest for you to feel?
6. Which positive one was easiest for you to feel?
7. Explain any difference you felt in the various positive energies.

Why was that feeling exercise so important? Because, if you have any intention whatsoever of taking charge of your life, you *must* be able—at any given moment—to know what kind of vibrations you're sending out. If you can *feeeeel* what you're flowing in any moment, you can take charge of your life. If you can't, or don't care to, then you'll stay on unhappy autopilot until you check outta here.

Principle #2   We attract according to how we are feeling

We've said it before, we'll say it again and again and again: The way we feel regulates the kind of vibrational *frequency* that flows from us. Whether a high feel-good or low feel-bad frequency, it's all highly magnetic and will attract its like, whether *we* like it or not! *Because like frequencies attract!* Pure physics.

Low, slow "social consciousness" vibrations (from negative feelings) attract only low, slow, fear-based stuff like lack, struggle, pain, suffering, etc.

High, fast "greater Self" vibrations (from positive feelings) attract only high, fast, happy kinds of things, or people, or places, or events—things that will make you happy because they feel good.

o We struggle because of how we're feeling/flowing/vibrating

o We get rich because of how we're feeling/flowing/vibrating

o We get sick because of how we're feeling/flowing/vibrating

o We meet people because of how we're feeling/flowing/vibrating

o We get *everything* because of how we're feeling.

> There is not one thing in life that comes to us by any means other than from the magnetic vibrations of the feelings that we send out all day long. Not one, ever! Cosmic Physics.

The Match 'em Up Exercise

The moment—the moment—you can connect real events of your past with how you were flowing your energy (feelings) prior to the happening, you're well on your way to being a deliberate creator, meaning you'll start creating by intent rather than by goof-up.

List "biggies" from your past, good or bad events or periods of time you'll never forget, and try to recall how you were feeling in the months, days, or years prior to the event. If it was just a little fender-bender, you don't have to go back very far. If it was a divorce, go back further. If you went bankrupt, go back quite a ways. I beg you, be honest with yourself. Cut away all denial, and take a long hard look at your predominate moods prior to—and even during—the happening. Were you frightened, bored, happy, worried, excited, angry? For now, stay out of your childhood. If you're stuck, do the LEFT side first, then chew on the answers.

Event	Predominate mood(s) prior to that event
The god-awful year I was flat dead broke	scared to death for months before. Depressed, feeling like a failure.

Discuss and/or Journal

1. Did you fill up the page?
2. If not, why not? (Resistance? Disbelief?)
3. Which matchup was most obvious to you? Why?
4. Do you still feel others were to blame? Explain.
5. Were any of the events tied to old beliefs? Explain.
6. Is there a pattern you can see? Describe it.
7. If not, try to find a pattern, and describe it.

Please! Don't skimp. Take one at a time. Think about it, feel it, and do all you can to LEARN from how you answered.

The bottom line to this is that when you were feeling good, good things happened. When you were feeling bad, poopy things happened. But remember, feeling bad doesn't have to mean you're in the sewer. A "feel-bad" flow of energy is anything from flatlining (where you *think* you're feeling nothing), to mild worry or concern, to terror, whereas a "feel-good" flow of energy is anything from gentle appreciation to ecstasy.

Tune in to your feelings!

o There is only one thing that has anything to do with what we are getting, and that is how we are flowing our energy.

o Frustrated? Discouraged? Justifying? Rationalizing? Those feelings are indicators that we are flowing our energy nonproductively.

o Got hurt feelings? What someone said has nothing to do with us, only what they are attracting into *their experience*, and we happened to walk into it.

o Learn to observe through feelings, not your head.

o We are flow-ers of energy! Unless we're feeling terrific, we're flowing negative energy.

- Every moment we spend feeling negative emotion, we deprive ourselves of the life force that is natural to us, heals us, and magnetizes our desires.

- Instead of thinking about it, feel about it.

- If we want to change the conditions of our lives, we must change our vibrations, meaning feelings.

- Don't try to label it, just tune in to how it feels: good, lousy, or blank.

- Life is about feeling. Learn to feel, good or bad, up or down, and the doors to the treasures of the universe will open to you.

Principle #3   What we focus on is what we get

Focus on something that makes you feel bad, and you draw to you "feel-bad" things that cause you to feel *just like the frequency you sent out.* Focus on something that makes you feel good ... same thing.

If you can reach in and *feeeeel* even a little tiny bit of emotion about something when you're thinking about it, you'll know in a flash how you're flowing your energy and how you're attracting.

> Once you've made the simple association between how you feel and how you're flowing energy, the world becomes your oyster.

The Negative Game

It's never about what we're thinking when we draw stuff to ourselves; it's only about what we're *feeeeeling*.

All day long we flow our energy—meaning we feel—in a way we think is perfectly normal, when all the while we're attracting the opposite of our desires. This is just pretend, but play the game anyhow. You'll soon see how our focus attracts.

The object of our focus (What we've been pondering)	The result of our focus (A likely outcome of that energy)
All you can think about is your empty bank account	
The TV is filled with news of a deadly new bacteria	
You keep seeing—everywhere—the new car you want	
You're terrified of being attacked or mugged	
You're going to change jobs because you hate your boss	
You're afraid of being fired, downsized, laid off	
You're afraid this new love will be just like the last	
It's burn season, and you're worried about your home	
You detest nasty waitresses	

continued . . .

The object of our focus (What we've been pondering)	The result of our focus (A likely outcome of that energy)
You know education has held you back	
You hate to wait in line	
You deeply resent the IRS	
You forever wish your spouse would stop doing "that"	
The barking dog next door is driving you nuts	
You're embarrassed by your old car	
The teachers in your kids' school are too progressive	
Being alone makes you depressed	
You're concerned that your memory is failing	
You hate your work	
Your looks aggravate you . . . a lot	
You're "for" it, but you know the group's against it	
You've always wished you could do "that" better	
You never really felt the deal would go through	

feel bads →

Closed Valve

Imagine that you're connected to a fire hose, and *you* are the nozzle. The hose connects you with the pure, positive energy of life, the real You, All That Is, your expanded Self. When you close down the nozzle to pinch off the full stream of energy (you can't shut it off completely or you'd be outta here), you're into negative emotions. So begin to think in terms of:

"Is my valve open, or closed?"

Writing around the circle (as below), list several other times (different from what's on your Match 'em Up List) when bad things happened to you. This is just another reminder that you were operating with a closed valve when they happened, perhaps still plugged into old negative beliefs.

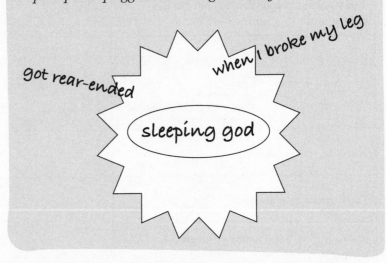

got rear-ended

when I broke my leg

sleeping god

During our day, if we would change just three negative thoughts (Closed valve feelings) out of 100, the high-frequency energy we pull in is so powerful, it would automatically change the low-frequency energy that's at the core of the other 97! In other words, it doesn't take much to turn our lives around. We don't have to watch every little feeling and thought. We only have to consciously decide we're going to change as many as possible. "How does this feel? Am I ready to change the feeling? How am I flowing my energy? Is my valve open, or closed?"

feel goods →

Open Valve

Our natural state is feeling good, but to be there we have to stay out of our habitual feelings of lack. Since what we're vibrating is our point of attraction, it would behoove us to learn to *intentionally* feel good, where our valve is open to our own natural energy. Doubt restricts the flow, creating a Closed valve. Joy, excitement, appreciation, awe, love, and reverence all speed the flow. Now our valve is open, and we are receiving our own natural flow of high-frequency energy. This is our natural state, but one we must learn to cultivate for as long as we're on this planet.

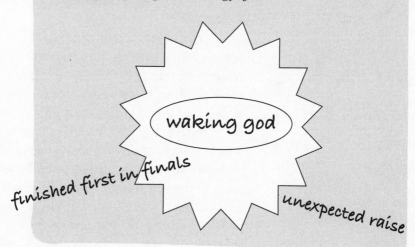

Write out the times when something GOOD happened. That's when you had your valve open, were feeling good and flowing the pure, positive energy of You.

waking god

finished first in finals

unexpected raise

Closed valves = tough lives; open valves = prosperous lives.

Principle #4   Deliberate creation must be planned

We are electromagnetic beings, attracting events, people, places, and things to us by the vibrations we emit. Those vibrations, either high and fast from positive, valve-open, happy feelings or low and slow from negative, valve-closed, bummer feelings, flow out from us every minute of every day to find their matching frequencies and magnetize them back to us.

We attract what our attention is turned to, because that sets up our magnetic vibrations. And the thought form that's created by our constant attention to something just grows and grows and grows. The more we think about it, the bigger and stronger (magnetically) it gets. If it's a belief we've had for a lifetime, it's big. If it's our poor financial state that we've been in for ages, it's big. So how do we turn around a lifetime of negative thoughts that we consider normal? How do we blast away generations of negative beliefs about blame and persecution and lack and luck and unworthiness?

> When you are in a place of focusing on what makes you feel good, you are in a place of deliberate, positive creation. You are in control of your life.

First, remember that creating is vibrating. The happier you are, the neater the things you're going to attract. Next, remember that you can't have it both ways; you can't be thinking about lack and expect to have divine assistance. But when you vibrate in a place of joy, you and your inner being are vibrating together. You're in sync with that greater You, which is why it feels so good to feel good.

Above all else, start paying attention to how you feel. The most important thing you can do in a day is to deliberately flow energy that feels good. If you're flatlining (nothing happening, nothing moving, and no feeling either way, which is pretty much our usual state), you're attracting negatively. Get the energy flowing. Get your frequencies up.

Each hour, for just a few minutes, decide to feel good about something. Anything! If you will do that each hour for only sixteen seconds at a time, without *any* negative input, you will begin to alter the entire vibrational patterning of your being without having to dig at old beliefs or watch everything you say or think. See yourself as a magnet, and learn to feel.

Thoughts that are similar to each other are magnetically drawn together. When you think about something that pleases you, other thoughts with the same vibration will be attracted to that pleasing thought. Like attracts like. The universe doesn't hear your words, only your vibrations. And so, when you are in a place of focusing on what makes you feel good, you are in a place of deliberate, positive creation. You are in control of your life. You are in tune with your expanded Self.

In a yucky circumstance? It's your vibration that's put you there. Want to get out of it? Then it's time to change your vibrations and implement the awesome power of You. Learn to open your valve. Learn to act only by feeling. Learn to ask yourself, in every moment, *"How do I feel? Is my valve open, or closed?"*

The Four Steps of Deliberate Creation

Deliberate creating is nothing more than the purposeful directing of the pure, positive, high-frequency vibrations that come from feel-good thoughts.

Step One: *Identify what you don't want.*

Step Two: *From that, identify what you do want.*

Step Three: *Get into the feeling place of your want.*

Step Four: *Intend—and allow—it to happen.*

That's all there is to it. Simple, but not easy. We have a lifetime of what we've considered to be "normal" feelings to change. We have generations of "normal" thinking, reacting, blaming, struggling to change. We even have our own need to be in pain to change. But the good news is we *can* do it, simply by changing how we think in any one moment, which changes the way we feel, which changes our frequency, which changes the way we vibrate, which changes the way we attract.

Fun Ways to Prove:

How like frequencies attract
See if you can find two or three tuning forks that are each of a different pitch. For instance, one might be tuned to A, another to E, etc. (You might borrow these from a school's music department.) You'll need at least two of different pitches so that they vibrate at different frequencies. Ping one, and see if the other pings too. *(It won't, because only like frequencies attract.)*

How magnetic our feeling-thoughts are
Take two wire coat hangers and make two "Ls." The handle will be about 5" long, the pointer almost a foot. Hold them by the handles as if pointing two six-shooters, but very loosely. Now think about something *ugly* from your past, then something *happy* in your future, and watch what happens. Think *lovingly* about something to your left, and watch what happens. Think *lovingly* about something in back of you, and watch. Play with your deep feeling-thoughts, and you'll soon see how magnetic you really are.

> When we raise our frequencies, magic happens.

Becoming God-consciousness

As you go inside to that still, quiet place of knowing, imagine yourself at the center of a vast hourglass of liquid white light. Its top extends beyond time into the next universe, and its bottom reaches into and wraps the core of Mother Earth. Intensify the luminosity, and fill it with a frequency of deep, deep love while you continue to feel yourself at the apex, assisting in the creation of the raising of the consciousness of humankind.

When you are ready, place into that limitless light the frequency of appreciation. Let it flood through you from the heavens into the earth. Hold that vibration for as long as you can, or want to.

Now allow the frequency of gratitude to fill the funnel, and hold it for as long as you can. Truly, for as long as you can.

> **INSIGHT**
> The higher our frequencies, the greater out light; the greater our light, the stronger our power.

Now put yourself into the frequency of reverence, or awe, as if looking over the Grand Canyon, or viewing earth from afar. Hold the feeling . . . hold the feeling . . . hold the feeling.

And now see and feel your divine hourglass of effervescent light fill with profound love . . . love for humankind . . . love for this blessed planet . . . love for those who walk with you . . . and love for you. Let it wash throughout every inch of your body, every cell of your being, every atom of the highly magnetized air about you. Take time . . . allow yourself to *feeeeel* the feelings. Take time; no rush.

And now, feel the joy that fills your body and being. Give yourself time to feel . . . and be . . . and when you're ready, come on back. You have infused high frequencies of joy into this world, and into yourself.

Ask to expand.

Ask to be filled with those things
the soul longs for.

You are given nothing until you ask.
When you ask of the divine within you,
you become the divine within you.

Tenet Four

We giggle at why we are here

Principle #1   The soul hungers for what it has never experienced

What are we doing here? Is there a purpose? Is life predestined? Bottom line: Is there a reason, or did we just pop in by some fluke?

It might annoy you a tad to find out that earth was created as a playground for the gods. Really! This place that our unseen friends call "the jewel of the universe" was originally designed as a vast cosmic library where every single thing that had ever been created, or a portion of that thing, would be placed to be archived forever more. At the same time, since all the goodies of the universe would be here, what a fun experience it would be to go through a lifetime or two here, in this very different place, to further the soul's growth.

Good idea, but it backfired. Over eons, the place became so popular, any idea of "playground" went by the wayside as groups struggled to live in a sometimes hostile arena. Yet oddly enough, the greater the struggles grew, the more souls wanted to come. Why?! Why would a being choose to bip into a place that's in such apparent disharmony and fear and hate and lack? What would be the point?

There were a lot of us who continued to think we could come here and just have a good time, like having a rest between classes, so to speak. After all, it's still a unique sandbox to play around in. And in fact, a few *(very* few) will pop in each year to do just that: play. Lucky them! But for the vast majority of us, we're here at the beckoning of our soul, that little tiny spark tucked away just behind our heart. We call it the soul, but in fact, that little spark is why we are here.

This thing we call the soul is like a computer chip, designed exclusively to hold data in the form of emotions and feelings. It holds the emotional memory from every life we've ever lived and every experience we've ever had, from this lifetime back to our beginnings. It is the gigantic emotional memory bank of our being (for memory is emotion, not intellect), retaining all the happiness and pain that *has* been dealt with, and all that *has not.*

If we've never dealt with a particular pain, the soul presses us to experience something similar again in order to own it. If we have a yen to do something or go somewhere (like Egypt, not the grocery store), then the soul needs a particular emotional experience to fill the requirements of its emotional treasure hunt. Something is still missing to complete its journey. When you go against a strong desire or yearning to experience something... well, we call that despair, depression, sickness, neurosis, etc.

Either way, whether it's an old hurt or pain you've never owned and therefore need to experience again to put it to rest or a new type of emotion you've never experienced (from elation to terror), the soul will push the pants off you to get you into an experience that will, if you *own* it, satisfy the requirements set up by its original intent package. When that one's finished, the soul will take on another hunger, and you'll be propelled into a new adventure or new experience.

Now, here's the not-so-comfortable news: As you fuel your desire to turn to the light, the soul's activity increases proportionately. That little sucker knows where every tiny piece of your resistance is and will do everything in its power to pull you into experiences to blast open those areas of resistance. In other words, just by hungering for the light, which was a soul push, you've given the soul permission to do whatever is necessary to get you there.

If you need it, the soul will push you to experience it, again and again and again until you can say, "Oh happy days, I *GOT* it!!!"

The Strong Yens / Old Hankerings Exercise

We really are here to play, but since most of us haven't yet evolved to the point where we can do that, and that alone, we still have lessons to learn.

How many deep urges or longings or yens can you list that are probably the soul pressing you to dive into that emotional experience? What we're looking for here are things like, "I've always wanted to..." Now granted, if you can't carry a tune, being an opera singer might be a stretch, but even that kind of urge would have a counterpart of some kind, a reason for being within you. So list it.

Ignore the circles for now. ↓

I've always wanted to learn to fly	◯
1.	◯
2.	◯
3.	◯
4.	◯
5.	◯
6.	◯
7.	◯
8.	◯

If you've listed none, if you believe you have no urges, you are not being honest, for within the soul there is *always* more to garner. There's always more, and it's always better.

Discuss and/or Journal

1. If you listed only two or three yens, are you afraid to look at others?
2. Star the one you truly crave to do. You'll be coming back to it.
3. What do you think the chances are of your actually doing it?
4. What are the chances of your doing others?
5. Now go back and number them, in the circles and in pencil, in order of desire and place a one- or two-word description of that desire in the corresponding box below.

1.	2.
3.	4.
5.	6.
7.	8.

6. What is the pattern you see? Is "being by water" in the first three boxes? Is it travel? What's important and what isn't? What matches and what doesn't? Do they all have to do with a home or a lover or airplanes or animals? Or only some? How many patterns can you find? Discuss and/or journal in detail. This will become very important as we go on.

Principle #2 We come in with some basic lessons

We pop in here with two or three major things the soul wants us to get this time around, plus a few more tossed in for good measure, things we didn't get the last time around or even countless times before that. Since the purpose of life is to learn through exploration, adventure, and pleasure, when we turn it all into pain and struggle, the soul—with the exuberant cooperation of our entity—does whatever it takes to get us into learning the lesson and out of our rut. And by the way, *we* make the decision as to what we're going to work on in each lifetime, not the soul. Our soul only lays out options. It is not the dictator.

Maybe you felt you needed to work on separation this time around, or guilt, or to experience fame, or smooth out self-worth issues. The soul will set those vibrations in your energy field to magnetize events that will give you the opportunity to get whatever needs to be experienced.

Before you come in here, you've laid out a basic game plan. That's all! No predestiny, no karma, just, "Well, I didn't get it last time, so I'll see if I can set it up another way this time." Then, before you take off, you and a whole bunch of your friends have agreed, actually contracted, to do various things to help each other out with your respective lessons—even to dying, rape, or murder.

> When you find out what you're doing here, being here gets to be a whole lot more fun.

Let's say, for instance, you chose separation to be your number one issue. How could you tell? Well, if you've had many people who were close to you die, then it's a good guess that separation is one of the three biggies for you. Perhaps one or more of your children dies prematurely, or a beloved spouse. This was most likely a prearranged contract to help you understand there is no such thing as separation, that life is ongoing, that perpetual grief is an excuse not to live, and that you *can* grow into a feeling of wholeness without loved ones in your life.

If you can look at the world through understanding glasses that reveal the lessons of friends, lovers, partners, co-workers, leaders, countries (yes, countries have lessons too), and children, then your perspective and your vibrations will change markedly, for the horrendously destructive energy of judgment will be gone from you now and for all time to come.

If you can discover even one or two of the major things you came here to "get" and put to bed for all time, you'll be giving yourself a huge leg up, because you'll begin to see your games and know how to change them. When you find out what you're doing here, being here gets to be a whole lot more fun.

Think of asking and receiving as the same thing. If you say, "Throw me the ball," you have already affirmed you are ready to receive it.

Can-You-See-It Exercise

If we can see it in others we can more easily spot and deal with it in ourselves.

Seeing the games that other people play is usually a lot easier than seeing our own. So let's start there . . . with other folks. Anybody, whether they're friends or not. The boxes below are headed with various circumstances, or appearances, in one's life. Jot down what some of the related lessons might be for you or anyone. Don't worry which would be the most important; that's not for us to decide. What IS important is the awareness that everyone from Hitler to Hussein is working on lessons, and always in cocreation.

Constantly broke	Successful businessperson
Negativism	
Need for phony identity	
No concept of God-self	
Not aware we create our reality	

Partner-hopper	Failed businessperson

continued . . .

Incessant braggart	Big rock/tv/movie star

Politician	Low self-esteem

One who steals	Substance abuser

Make your own headings.

Repetitious Patterns Exercise

Now it's time to find out what *your* lessons might be. The easiest way to do that is to list those things, or habits, in your life you've repeated over and over again. For instance: new job, but same kind of boss. New lover, but same kind of problems. Fired often, diet often, move often, have accidents often.

Create four separate headings out of those unfortunate events that seem to constantly repeat themselves in your life and put them in the gray areas. Then list the possible lessons.

Don't rush this one; think it through!
↓

A Repetitious Pattern of Mine Is:	A Repetitious Pattern of Mine Is:
Possible Lessons Are:	Possible Lessons Are:

A Repetitious Pattern of Mine Is:	A Repetitious Pattern of Mine Is:
Possible Lessons Are:	Possible Lessons Are:

Lessons

Lessons Exercise

Okay, you've seen some of your repetitious patterns and listed some of their potential lessons. Now let's narrow it down even more to find the recurring lessons. Pick any lesson and put it in Square One. Let's say the lesson is self-worth. Look over your "Possible Lessons" from the previous page and see if you can find ones that are similar, like shame or insecurity or shyness.

Any one lesson	Similar types	Similar types	Similar types	Similar types	Similar types
1.					
2.					
3.					
4.					
5.					
6.					

Now finish the job! Put the lessons with the most similar types into the Major column, and the rest in the Minor one.

Probably the main lessons I came here to learn are:

Major	Minor
1.	1.
2.	2.
3.	3.

Discuss and/or Journal

1. How did you feel about the repetitious patterns that showed up on the previous page?
2. Were you aware you had these patterns? Explain.
3. If you were not aware of them, how do you feel about them now?
4. From this page, discuss the trends you found that might weave themselves into a major lesson.
5. Does seeing them make you unhappy or discouraged?
6. What's the biggest thing you've learned from these two exercises?

Principle #3 All issues are lessons

Before we go any further into the sometimes boring topic of lessons, it's important we remember who and what we are and why we're here. Yes, "remember," because believe me, you *do* know. First, we are eternal beings of light, ongoing immortal "pinch-offs" of whatever Source we came from (there are many Sources). Some of us were created just for physicality; some of us were created for—and come from—other realities. One is not better than the other.

But whatever reality or Source we come from, not only are we learning to clear away "normal" issues so that we might grow into the totality of our being (as all of humanity is doing and has done since it began), but there's something more. Much more! A group we'll call "The Point Gang" is being pushed by their soul's blueprint into something that has never been accomplished—ever.

A small group of us, including you, volunteered to be part of the group who are here to pave the way for all of humankind to eventually become an individuated Self that shall be more—that's right, *more* than the Source from which it came. That human shall be a Self, a Creator, and a Source, all in one. It has never happened before.

Not an easy job, and not always a fun one. Pioneers are out on an edge, asking for trouble while at the same time finding a thrill in the risk. They're the ones who trip the most, lose their way, and get cut by the entangling brush. But something keeps them going. Not an elite group, not a special group, just a bunch of hopelessly driven volunteers with an unspeakable, indefinable passion. Like it or not, by the simple virtue of your involvement with this guidebook, you are one of those pioneers.

Lessons, for anyone on this path today, are coming fast with big wallops. Security blankets are being pulled out from under us (and everybody) everywhere we turn. But the thing is, the sooner *we* get what our lessons are all about, the sooner mankind will get the message too. So the push is on for us to get what we came here to get, because every time *we* get it, social consciousness rises. Every time *we* own a past issue or let go of an old sore or stop another old game dressed up with new players—every single time we make a shift in *us*—we make a shift in the mass consciousness.

While every issue we have is a lesson of some sort, what's more important is that when we're into issues, no matter how small or petty, we're into—and magnetizing more—low-frequency energy. So everything we do from here on in will be about dumping issues, clearing lessons, and bringing us into a state of "life is good, people are good, and all is well with me and mine." That's called joy!

"Issues" are always negative energy.

HOMEWORK: *Issue-feeling*

Issues are lessons, and lessons are issues, but since issues seem more "everyday" to us, we can often spot them easier than big old lessons.

Keep a running list of the things you have issues with, no matter how small. As you list each one, simply note down how that feeeeels *to you. It won't be long before it will be fairly obvious why doing away with issues would be a really fine idea!*

I sort of, kind of, or really have an issue with . . .	Thinking about it makes me feel . . .
People who bike with dogs not on a leash	Furious!

Principle #4   We cannot find the light until we acknowledge the darkness

This is called *owning*!

Owning is:

o Taking hold of your past, and owning it all

o Welcoming your past, and owning it all

o Knowing no one's responsible but you

o Getting rid of if-onlys

o Knowing you can create it any old way you want it

o Stopping stuffing

And Owning is:

o Insisting on finding and feeling the emotion behind any event

o Accepting you did what you did for the emotional experience of it

o Getting off your case, like *now*

o Realizing you never made a mistake

o Giving up guilt…for good!

o Not regretting one single thing you ever did

> Until we own it, we'll repeat it!

Until we own it all, every hurt feeling, every piece of guilt or shame, every resentment, all the pain, and all the disapproval of ourselves (not to mention of everyone else), we can only flow low-frequency energy every day of our lives. That energy flows out from us, attracting more unpleasant experiences until we finally get the message that we still haven't owned the emotion. We need only allow ourselves to feel the stuffed guilt or hate or whatever one last big time, then let the bloody thing go! Owning is releasing that negative energy.

Explanation Break

"I've taken a lot of inventories and gotten rid of a lot of stuff. Why is it so important to do any more now? What's really the big deal about Owning?"

The actual physics of owning, meaning what happens to you as a result of owning, are astronomical. Remember, the way we think causes the way we feel, and the way we feel causes the way we attract.

Until we clear them, lessons sit in our energy field (the light field which surrounds our bodies, also called the aura) as little blobs of electromagnetic energy. Those blotches are highly charged with whatever energy (negative or positive) is necessary to draw to us the circumstances required for us to gain the emotional wisdom of the lesson. And they'll stay there, drawing new people, places, or things into our lives until we've owned the lesson.

> You have nothing to lose but your unhappiness.

The same is true of any kind of issue, which is also a form of lesson. The more we think about the issue, the stronger we feel about it. The stronger we feel about it, the more of it we attract!

But now look what happens when we learn the lesson within one of those black blotches. The energy of that particular lesson, or issue, is instantly dissipated, meaning we won't be attracting it again! Our valve opens a bit more, making it possible for us to feel—and attract—far more positively.

All it takes is a decision to stop thinking about an issue and own the fool thing, admit you were a dork, and move on. But if you continue to get a rush from crucifying yourself—or someone else—for past actions, remember this: All things are done in cocreation. If it was done *to* you, you agreed to it—from another level—to experience whatever lesson was up for you. If you did it to someone else, same thing. You both always did what you did to learn something.

So if you want to open your valve and move on ... get off your case, give it up, let the damn thing go!

"Owning" Inventories

We've done "Blame." We've done "Issues." We've done "If-Onlys". Now let's see if we can clean this lesson business up once and for all with old regrets, guilts, mistakes, failures, hates, resentments, anything you know darn well you've been hanging on to all these years, and any other thing or person not yet forgiven.

Maybe you've already listed some of these. That's okay, list them again here. If you find overlaps in categories, put them where the feelings seem the strongest. Dip into your past (far back or recent), and feeeeel what you're still hanging on to. The categories are separated to push you into thinking about them, rather than keeping them stuffed. Note that "Resentments" take up most of the spaces. That's because they are the easiest for us to feel and recall. To the degree you feel comfortable doing so, discussing any of these items in a group will be beneficial to all.

Things I've Regretted: Not telling my folks I was an addict

Guilts: For saying those things to Sam just before he died

continued . . .

Big Mistakes I've Made: Investing in that dumb gold mine

Failures:

Boiling Hates:

Resentments:

Calling it forth

Please read this meditation through carefully before beginning. It will place a strong vibration of "intent" into your field that you may or may not want to have there. The intent is that you shall now bring forth into your world the experiences of all lessons you have not yet dealt with, and of all issues yet to be owned and cleared.

Go to your special place before beginning, someplace where you can be alone to feel the utmost reverence for you. Call to your entity, those who walk with you, and all loving universal energies to assist you. Go inside, raise your frequencies by loving, and then center. Know that the words you are about to utter will change your life forever.

And now, say out loud with purposeful intent, "From the Light of God that I Am, I call forth unto my world all lessons and learning that I have not yet allowed myself to experience. I ask, in fact I insist, that all such lessons be drawn to me in the vibration of peace, never in the pain of unaware chaos. "I ask that those who walk with me help me to see the lessons in the experiences to come so that I can find the healing and the fulfillment I so deeply desire to have.

"I fervently ask that if I do not immediately allow myself to feel and own the emotions of the lesson— no matter how painful that emotion may be—that I be lovingly shown how to allay my anxieties in order to allow the experience of fully owning the emotions.

> **INSIGHT**
> When we call forth and own all that remains to be cleared, we will know joy.

"I call this forth in the name of That Which I Am, in the full knowing that as I have spoken, so it shall be. So be it. "

Take several long moments to feel a sense of excitement and anticipation for what you have just done. No step shall ever be bigger, no call ever more joyously received in the heavens than this. You are greatly loved . . . and treasured . . . and adored. Feel it, and come back.

Didn't you ever feel that there's some secret part of you that knows everything there is to know but just doesn't stick its head out? There is.

Tenet Five

We welcome, even invite contrast

WITH THIS TENET WE

- o learn to identify what we don't want

- o explore the disaster of negative emotions

- o examine Step One of the Law of Attraction

- o learn how to be observers rather than responders

Principle #1   Contrast gives us choices

Most of us think we'd eagerly give up the crud in our lives for peace and quiet, ease and harmony. We'd order up, "Good life only, please; hold the pain."

Well, believe it or not, contrast is why we came here. Any realm that is three-dimensional, as ours is, functions in duality, so everything is either this or that, up or down, male or female, left or right, black or white, good or bad, right or wrong. Our problem has been one of focus, in constantly seeing only things we don't want, rather than learning to flow our energies to those things we do want.

"Don't worry, I'll get it this time," we say courageously before coming in. But once here, we get so caught up in the low vibrations of social consciousness, we completely forget we are actually power centers of energy, creating in every moment more and more of what we don't want just by our attention to it. We forget we have the power to choose. Instead, as we fall in step with humanity's negative energy, we begin the lifelong litany of Don't Wants, flowing more and more energy to those things we dislike and attracting more of the same. We think we're stuck with it all, so rather than exercising our right of choice and saying, "Don't want this, so I think I'll choose that," we shrug, "Hells bells, I don't want this, but guess I'm stuck."

Contrast gives us the opportunity to find out what we don't want, so we can call in what we do want. Our job, then, becomes one of change of focus, of taking our closed-valve fixation *off* what we *don't want*, and flipping it open to what we *do want. We cannot be deliberate creators without contrast.* So bless it all, invite it in, and know that before too long, the contrast that is all around you will become a no-thing as you learn the incredible powers you have to use.

Principle #2   All "Don't Wants" feel bad

Contrast gives us choice, without which we'd have no desire to create a change. Contrast is the primary force behind deliberate creation. "Sure don't want this, so I'm definitely choosing that." Bang! We're deliberately creating.

Until we know we have choices, we either stagnate or try getting what we want by physically whacking our desires into place, which rarely works. The only way we can materialize our Wants is to flow opened valve energy that feels good, rather than closed valve, negative energy that feels bad. And all Don't Wants feel bad, no matter what kind.

So the first thing we're going to do is nail down the difference in feeling between a Want and a Don't Want. No, that's not as simpleminded as it may sound, for Don't Wants are far more pervasive, far more all-encompassing, and far more sneaky than you may think. In fact, this entire Tenet is about Don't Wants, the first step in the Law of Attraction.

The Law of Attraction
Step #1: Identify What You Don't Want

But what does "feeling bad" really mean? It can mean anything from no feeling at all to despondency and everything in between. And with every Don't Want you focus on, you are flowing more closed valve, negative energy out to attract more of the same. Feeling bad is what we do all day long, and we think it's normal. Feeling bad is looking with constant focus on Don't Wants.

Don't Wants . . .

o   are always negatively charged

o   can be problems, issues, or conditions we don't like

o   are what we focus on for 98 percent of our day

o   are not permanent; only our focus holds them to us

Don't Wants are how we view the world, and they . . .

o never feel good when we think about them

o never feel like a warm fuzzy

o feel perfectly normal to us

o feel no different than what we think life is

Don't Wants are always with us, unless consciously dissipated.
You can be a sweet, kind, and "good" person; you can be a
goodie-two-shoes or a first-class people-pleaser; you can be
deeply religious; you can be a grand philanthropist; but if you're
not happy, having fun, enjoying life to the hilt, having a ball,
and basically feeling great, you're living from Don't Wants.

Any negative focus
is a Don't Want.

Feeeeel the Difference Exercise

**(This exercise is continued with "Don't Wants/Wants" on the follow-
ing pages.)**

**Until we can feel the difference between a Want and a
Don't Want, we're flying blind, creating by chance rather
than choice. Or put another way, flow bummer feelings,
get bummer results.**

How does something make you feel when you talk about it?
Warm fuzzies? Happy? Tickled? Upbeat? If not, your valve
is closed, and you're magnetizing everything into your life
except the things you want. The universe only responds to
what we're flowing out, not what we're wishing for. And the
only way we can know for sure how we're flowing is by how
we're feeling while we're thinking about something. Feel
good? It's on its way! Feel bad? It's on its way. No feeling at
all? Then no movement at all.

What we're thinking/*feeeeling* and what we're getting are
always a match. Always. It's the first law of physics: like attracts like. Flow it out, get it back! So here's what we're going to do (on the next pages):

1. On the first page, list those Don't Wants you've
   already been through (or you're into now) that you
   are tired of repeating or would like to get rid of.

2. List only five at a time, but do *not* get into their feelings … yet.

3. When you've listed five Don't Wants, go over to the right-hand page and list what you want instead. **IMPORTANT!! Never mind that you think it could never happen or you can't afford it or it's just daydreaming. Forget all that and just write it down. We'll get to the business of believability later.**

4. Now! Go back to your first Don't Want and *feeeeel* what it feels like down to the core of your being! You've already been there, so you know how yucky it feels, but do it anyhow. Make yourself get into it. Hold it for 30 seconds … check off the appropriate feeling box, then instantly move over to your corresponding Want, and experience the thrill, the freedom, the joy, the exhilaration, the happiness of that. **Forget about it being an impossibility!** *Feeeeel* it, and fill in the boxes. Do 30 seconds each side, or longer if you can.

5. Now do five more. Do as many as you possibly can in the first sitting. This is too important to postpone. It is, in fact, the crux of what you will be doing for the rest of your life if you desire to become a deliberate creator.

6. Please note: Make a clear distinction between your feeling tones, meaning do *not* retain any of the Don't Want energy in your Wants. Separate them! Make them different. Your Don't Wants will feel bad (or have no feeling at all), and your Wants *must* feel juicy-good to you. If they don't make you giddy, or feel like warm fuzzies, or make you feel happy and safe, you're not yet into the feeling of the Want.

7. On the two pages after that, do the same thing, only this time with things in the future you don't want to have happen. Don't Wants (and Wants) can be planetary (common to all), or big personal (really important stuff), or little personal (like frogs in Junior's pocket). It doesn't matter, put them all down. Until we see how often we focus negatively, about everything, our lives will never change. Have fun!

continued …

Don't Wants

Don't Wants I've already experiencd, or am still experiencing, and don't want to experience again	Feels yucky	Not much feelin'	I focus on this a lot, some, rarely

Wants

Wants I'd like to experience instead of those Don't Wants (opposite page)	Feels great	Feels how?	I focus on this a lot, some, rarely

The future →

Don't Wants

Don't Wants I don't want to happen in the future, for me, my family, and/or the planet.	Feels yucky	Not much feelin'	I focus on this a lot, some, rarely

Wants

Instead of those future Don't Wants (opposite page), I'd like me (or my family or the planet) to experience . . .	Feels great	Feels how?	I focus on this a lot, some, rarely

Discuss and/or Journal

The Present

1. How easy was it for you to feel the Don't Wants?
2. Was feeling the Don't Wants easier than feeling the Wants? Explain in as much detail as you can.
3. Why do you think that is?
4. How hard was it for you to list your Wants?
5. Were there some Wants you could feel more easily than others? As you explain, see if you can identify what might have held you back.
6. Did you feel resistance to getting into the Wants feelings? Why?
7. Look at your Present Don't Want list, and add up the "Feels yucky" and "Not much feelin'" columns. Which has more checks, "Feels yucky" or "Not much feelin'"?
8. What would you deduce from that? (That you allow yourself to feel deeply? Or don't want to feel? Or there's just not much to it? What else?)
9. Can you see a pattern in what *kind* of Don't Want feels worse than another? If you do, explain why you think that is.
10. What kind of Want was it hardest for you to get into?
11. Now add up the different degrees of how often you focus on a Don't Want topic ("a lot," "some," "rarely"). What kind of Don't Wants do you focus on a lot? Why do you think that is?
12. Now add up the different degrees of how often you focus on a Want topic. Do you notice a major difference? What is it?

The Future

1. First, answer the same questions as above. Then answer the following ones:
2. Did you finish the Future Wants list? If not, what do you think might be going on? Take a really good stab at your answer!

3. What kind of Future Wants have you focused on the most?
4. Are you surprised by anything you put on either list, or by any kind of pattern that showed up?

The secret to magnetizing anything we want, from good health to abundant bank accounts to great relationships, is nothing more than flowing energy from us that feels good instead of bad. Go back to these pages as often as you can. Practice!!! Fill in more, and *feeeeel* more. Tune in to your body. Learn to tell the difference between a high and a low frequency. Take the time to *feeeeel* the change in energy between being fired and getting a raise or between holding a kitten or a poisonous snake. The vibrations are different because your feelings are different. Learn to tell the difference, and you will control your life.

> Don't Wants disconnect us from our Source.

Principle #3 All conditions result from energy flow

It doesn't matter whether it's something you like or not, if there's something in your life you're focusing on, you're making it bigger and drawing more of the same to you.

Don't Wants and conditions are actually the same thing, but we often respond to them differently. We tend to judge negative conditions far more harshly than our Don't Wants because we see ourselves as completely removed from them; therefore, they're fair game to judge. Starvation in Africa, poor reading techniques being taught in our schools, or being downsized into unemployment are examples of negative conditions. Yet the energy we flow *back out* as a result of our focus on the condition only makes the thing bigger and creates more of it. Around and around we go, which is why, for most of us, very little ever changes.

How-I-See-It Exercise

There are good conditions and bad conditions, those you like and those you don't. Some may be Don't Wants, but see if you can think of three for each category that you haven't listed before. In the first row, list three conditions you currently enjoy. In the second row, list three that don't matter to you. In the final row, list three conditions you truly hate or, at the very least, dislike. Those are the most glaring forms of contrast.

How do these conditions feel when you think about them?

"Love 'em"	"Who cares?"	"Awful stuff!"

How do these feel when you think about them?

As we observe, we attract.

Principle #4 Conditions don't mean diddly squat

Whatever problem we're into, whatever Don't Want is in our face, or whatever we see around us that we don't like doesn't mean a bloody thing; our *response* to it is all that matters. As long as we continue looking only at what *is*, we are attracting more of that by achieving vibrational harmony with it. Any negative situation is nothing more than an opportunity to decide what you *do* want, and then get on with it. (We'll find out how in the next couple of chapters.)

We are, unfortunately, far more aware of conditions—past, present, and potential—than we are of our own energy flow. So here are some one-liners to ease our way out of a negative focus and into empowerment.

o We're always going to respond to conditions, but we have a choice as to how: with an open valve or a closed one.

o If you don't like a condition, don't try to change it. Instead change either your focus or your energy, preferably both!

o The purer the energy we are flowing, the better we feel.

o The universe responds only to vibration, not words.

o As long as we hold a Don't Want in our vibration, we can never be a vibrational match to what we do want.

o The more we give our attention to the things we want to EXclude, the more we INclude them in our vibrations.

o The better we feel, the better things go; the worse we feel, the worse things go, because what we're focused on, we're flowing, and what we're flowing, we're attracting.

o Nothing affects our experience except our energy flow.

o When we can say, "I'm gonna keep my valve open regardless of the fool condition," we are incredibly free.

o The more open our valve, the sooner unwanted conditions will change or vanish or no longer matter.

o We are not here to be forever addicted to observing negative conditions; we are here to create our *own* experiences the way we desire them to be.

> As long as we're reacting to conditions,
> something will always be "wrong."

Principle #5 It takes only 16 seconds of focused thought to begin a manifestation

Can you imagine? Sixteen puny seconds is all we have to be thinking about something—*and flowing out the feeling energy coming from that thought*—and bingo! The manifestation process begins. Good stuff or bad, it doesn't matter. The feeling/thought goes out and forms a tiny vortex of energy. The more intense the emotion behind the thought, the more powerful the baby whirlpool of energy becomes, sucking in other thoughts just like it in emotion/frequency.

But now you give this thing you're thinking about another sixteen seconds of pure feeling without a moment of contradiction (it's either *all* negative or *all* positive), and it gets bigger, more powerful, more magnetic. Then you give it another sixteen seconds, and another, now you've got a "comer" on your hands. It's on its way, like it or not. If you've been flowing with a closed valve, you'll be attracting something negative; open valve, it'll be something positive. So if your "thing" has been a Don't Want, time to change your focus. Fast!

You can bang around for ten years disconnected and not accomplish what you can accomplish with one day of high, pure vibrations.

How I Grew My "Don't Want" Exercise

The actual exercise is on the next page. What's below is a sample.

Recall a MAJOR Don't Want in your life. Think back to when you first started thinking about it and when it started being a major point of focus until it finally manifested exactly as you hoped it would NOT! (This example is about a guy who got married in the 1980's, but had always worried about supporting a family.)

The years (from the beginning to the worst part)	When I'd think about it most (day night, work, etc.)	How much I thought about it during that period and what the intensity of feeling was	How it was beginning to get big in my life . . . then bigger, worse, out of control
1972	Don't remember	Not much, but some	
Mid-1980s	Watching Dad & Mom	Off and on, more than in the 1970s	
Early 1990s	At night, talking of having kids	A lot! Beginning to get really scared	Starting to overwork credit cards
Early 2000s	When our son was born	Worried about bills all the time	Bills getting really big
2005	I was laid off	Constant fear	Went bankrupt ... got divorced

continued . . .

This will give a very clear picture of how stuff comes to us. Be as detailed as possible so you can see the pattern of focus in progression. Remember, all it took to bring your Don't Want about was a series of sixteen seconds of concentrated focus and feelings. The more you thought about it, the bigger and stronger the spiraling vortex became, until you—and it—joined up as a vibrational match.

The years (from the beginning to the worst part)	When I'd think about it most (day, night, work, etc.)	How much I thought about it during that period, and what the intensity of feeling was	How it was beginning to get big in my life . . . then bigger, worse, out of control

Discuss and/or Journal

1. What part was most difficult for you? Explain.
2. Describe in some detail the progression of thought/feeling.
3. Having done this one, do you think you can see similar patterns of thought in your life that have produced similarly unhappy results?

So what really happened in our sample exercise that brought our hero's Don't Want crashing down upon him? It wasn't his upbringing or lack of education or his boss or spouse or kids or even his bills.

It was, quite simply, that one day (way back when) he saw a negative condition (lack of money in early family life). As he got older, he began to focus on it. And focus on it. And be worried about it happening to him. The die was cast.

The more he focused on his unwanted condition, the bigger the thought form became, fueled into greater magnetism by his emotions. This pulled his attention to it more and more, creating a vicious circle of negative thought, negative focus, and negative emotional flow.

With each sixteen seconds of negative emotion that poor guy would pour out, the little whirlpool thought form of lack he'd begun years before was becoming a highly charged time bomb. Not only was it beginning to pull in money problems, but it was now strong enough to pull in anything else that happened to be of the same resonance pattern. In our hero's case, it was bankruptcy and divorce, all from a constant focus on a potential condition he never wanted to experience!

> The worse we feel, the worse things get. The better we feel, the better things get.

But remember, just because you're not focusing on a Don't Want all day long doesn't mean you aren't flowing negative energy. Raising your frequencies takes focus. But you *can* do it, and before long you'll be looking at problems and be glad for them, or be in the middle of a crisis and know exactly what to do. Contrast, in all its forms, will become your most beloved ally. Without it, not one of us would ever know how to manifest a *truly* happy life!

Loving it away

Relax into that sacred, serene place of knowing within you ... that place where you are so very safe ... and free from all fears. Allow yourself to feel the love that wraps you in its arms.

As you settle in, pull up from the center of Mother Earth a stream of brilliant, shimmering emerald green light, and flow it right up through the base of your spine ... to your heart area. While the light dances about in your chest, place there—right in the middle of the light and your chest—one of your problems or negative conditions or Don't Wants.

> **INSIGHT**
> Whatever you want to remove in life, love it.

Now, turn the emerald green light of Mother Earth into the pure, white liquid light of All That Is, and surround your problem with this gift of your divinity. That light is pure love, so high in frequency, so filled with the God of You, the sweet problem in the middle will be altered forever.

Infuse every inch, every side drama of your problem with this light. Now bring up the intensity of the light, make it brighter with your love ... brighter with more love than you knew you had ... brighter yet with a love so filled with joy, and awe, and reverence, that you and the light become one.

As you continue to intensify the frequency around your problem, feel its preciousness, its vulnerability, its frantic struggle to survive. Tell your problem, in your own words, that it has done its job, and from the Light of God that you are, you thank it for its lessons and its pain. It has served you well, and now you are paying it honor.

Now as you hold the problem within the brilliant light, send it gently up and out through the top of your head, straight up, up, up, up, until you can just barely see it, and let it burst itself out in sparkles of joy into the heavens. You and your problem will never be the same, for you have loved it back into Life.

Tenet Six

We are learning to unleash our desires

- o learn to identify our Wants

- o initiate the lost art of dreaming

- o examine Step Two of the Law of Attraction

- o start the stubborn breaking down of "Want Barriers"

Principle #1   Wanting is our divine right

Once upon a time, back in the dark ages of our youth, it was okay to want—that is, until some huge adult told us we couldn't have the china vase to play with or pull the dog's tail or join the big kids in the street. "No, you don't want that" became the mantra of our subconscious.

As time went on and we continued our natural course of wanting in order to explore and experience every morsel of this bountiful new world, we soon faced a rude awakening. We'd want, not get, and feel the heavy pain of disappointment. It seemed like wanting was not a real spiffy thing to do.

Then we started our youthful religious teachings. If there had been any doubts before, there were none now. Wanting anything but the most mundane necessities was definitely out of the question. It was sinful. We were unworthy. God would punish us for our greed. It was better to give.

Put them all together, and by the time we reached some semblance of adulthood, most of us were basket cases about dreams and desires. Oh sure, the socially acceptable dreams were fine, like having a family, a job, success. But heaven forbid we should have desires apart from the norm. So we made sure whatever dreams we did secretly harbor were tidy and small, for two reasons: 1) so as not to offend that big roaring judge in the sky, and 2) so that if the dream didn't come to pass, we could handle the pain. "Dream small, hurt small" became our way of life.

That way of living is 100 percent opposite of what we were made for. Dreaming small is against our natural instincts, our divine nature. It is against cosmic law, for without large, outlandish dreams, we would not even be here.

Principle #2 "Want" is the first rule of empowerment

We're going to take this slow and easy, or we'll never get there. The barriers against wanting are too strong, too embedded in our psyches to go barreling ahead like we know what we're doing. Don't Wants are a piece of cake to us, but anything even smacking of fulfilling dreams is so foreign, and so frightening, we could blow this whole thing if we don't take it slow and easy. Like telling someone to get over their insecurities *today*. Good luck!

Some of the exercises in this chapter might feel repetitive, but they're not. They're designed with a gradual buildup to get us to where we can honestly say from the depths of our being, "By damn, I *want* that, and I intend to have it!" We are creator gods, born to create. Creating rules are in our spiritual as well as physical genetics. It is inherent in every fiber of our being, yet we cannot create without desire.

Even though Want and Desire are two sides of the same coin, the word "want" has such nasty connotations to it, such as need, greed, lack, and pain, that we use the word in only the most casual of conversations. But now we're going to change all that and learn to cut loose our Wants, because without those Wants we can never touch the glory of our beings. We can never fulfill our reason for being. We will never experience the thrill of exploration, the adrenaline rush of jumping into the unknown, or the divine pleasure born of a job well done.

We were created to create. Therefore, if divine empowerment is an earnestly sought-after Want, we'd better learn to want wholeheartedly, or empowerment will forever remain an unobtainable, discouraging, hurtful dream.

Sandcastle Exercise

Before diving in, we're going to play around in the shallow water and build some sandcastle foundations.

Inside each foundation block, jot down any ol' dream or desire you've always had, or even recently had, whether material, about people, or about you. Just list five of your most deeply held desires. There is no order of importance.

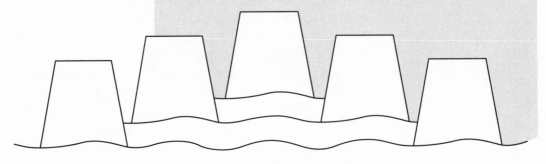

Want Barometer Exercise, Part I

This is *not* a "been there/done that" exercise. Yes, in the previous chapter you listed a whole barrelful of Wants, and you've just jotted down five Desires. These are NOT the same; we're now going *beyond* the surface stuff. You'll have to bypass your sense of unworthiness, your shame for being so greedy and self-centered, your fear of divine retribution, and any other no-no that comes to mind. I beg you, do not pass this over lightly. For all of its difficulty, this exercise is still only a bare beginning!

In the appropriate category (big, medium, minor Want), begin your list of Desires, or Wants, according to their degree of intensity. You can mix spiritual, material, physical, or emotional Wants in each category. The purpose here is to reprogram the brain into the first stages of knowing that Wanting is not only appropriate, but safe. As you go along,

continued . . .

you'll find how deeply your Wants are buried, and how hard it will be to pull them up. Be sure to put them in the proper category box according to the amount of desire you have behind them. And please, please, take your time and dig. Pull up all you can, then pull up more before leaving this exercise. I can't begin to tell you how important this exercise is. It's your life at stake. So please, dig!!!

Really, really want!

Sort of want

Just a passing thought

Discuss and/or Journal

Might as well settle down, as there's a bunch of things we need to learn from what we just did. Don't forget, the whole point here is to learn about ourselves in order to make changes. These segments give us the best opportunity to see where we're coming from and hopefully experience some "ah-ha"s as we discover things about ourselves we probably never realized.

Sandcastles

1. How hard was it for you to identify your five Sandcastle Wants?
2. Did you feel embarrassed as you wrote these down? Was there more embarrassment with one than with another? Dig deeply and explain.
3. Can you find—in those five—any sort of pattern? Are they all material or spiritual or about relationships? (There is no right or wrong!) Take a good hard look at the five, and describe the pattern.
4. Take each of the five, and identify the primary reason(s) you have not achieved this desire.
5. Having done that, was there a pattern in your reasons? Explain.

Want Barometer

1. Of the three levels of desire, which has the most empty spaces? Why is that?
2. In those that you listed as "sort of want," is that where they really belong? Would you secretly like to be thinking about any of those a whole lot more, but feel you shouldn't? Which ones? Explain.
3. Look at the Wants you listed in "Just a passing thought." Which of those would you really like to be dreaming about all the time?
4. In the "really, really want" group, what do you think are the primary reasons you haven't gotten them? (Don't worry, we'll come back to this to discover how to get rid of these "excuses.")

Want Barometer Exercise, Part II

We put the lid on most of our desires with social-consciousness "shoulds" and "shouldn'ts." We feel guilty, ashamed, unworthy, or undeserving. We feel that to want, rather than to give, is a sin, or unethical, or just flat-out selfish. And so our desires get stuffed.

Below and on the following page, take ten Wants from each category in your Want Barometer (or even from your Sandcastles), and assign each a number from one to five, five being the highest degree of feeling, under the appropriate column. For instance, if a "really, really want" is a lake house, but because of your finances you feel guilty every time you think about it, then note how guilty you feel, and assign it a number. Or how excited you allow yourself to feel. This exercise is primarily to expose our blocks to Wanting. We'll get to levels of excitement later.

WANT	Guilty, ashamed (1–5)	Unethical, sinful (1–5)	Unworthy, undeserving (1–5)	Discouraged (1–5)	Truly excited (1–5)
To be thin again					

continued . . .

WANT	Guilty, ashamed (1-5)	Unethical, sinful (1-5)	Unworthy, undeserving (1-5)	Discouraged (1-5)	Truly excited (1-5)
Be rich & famous					

Discuss and/or Journal

1. What did you discover overall?
2. Did you find you had more negative feelings in one category than in another? Do you think you can now explain why?
3. If you listed "excited" about any of your Wants, why do you suppose you don't have them yet, since excitement is the most powerful magnetic tool we have?
4. Was it hard for you to admit to having negative feelings about one or more of your Wants?
5. What patterns can you find, such as a lot of #5s in your "passing thought" category, or a lot of #1s in another category? What do those patterns tell you?

There are many, many more feelings we flow out when thinking about our wants and desires, but these will help you to see where you're coming from, and what kind of negative emotions have been holding those Wants away from you.

The point to these exercises is to show how great our need is to squelch our desires, whether from fear of disappointment or fear of disapproval or just our own feelings of unworthiness. Day in and day out, we deny ourselves our number one right...the right to any desire we may have.

Now granted, if your desire is to rule the world, and you couldn't care less how you get there, then we'd have a good argument in the works all about evil, right and wrong, etc. So when we talk about "your right" to have whatever your desire may be, let's not get hung up on moral semantics. That is not our issue here.

What we need to see is how easily and effortlessly we keep our happiness away from ourselves. We also need to see the excuses we usually chalk up to "reality." "Well, the reality is, I can't afford it." Or "the reality is I don't have the education." Or "the reality is it's just an impossible dream."

There is no "reality" that cannot or will not change, no matter how real it seems to us, but we have to give it something to change *to*. If all we ever feel when thinking about a want is some degree of shame or fear, the universe has no alternative but to bring us the match of that negative energy, called *struggle*!

Anything we allow to affect our vibration affects our manifestation. So here's the news flash: There is no dream, desire, or hankering that, when put into the proper vibrational flow, cannot be drawn into your reality and enjoyed to the fullest measure. Not one! *NOT ONE!!!* The universe has no standards for us. It will never withhold a thing from us or judge us in any way for our desires. The only thing that keeps our desire away is our own energy flow.

If we are to walk into empowerment, we must—repeat, *MUST*—get beyond the rights and wrongs of wanting. That is only social-consciousness nonsense. If what we come to receive makes us happy, then every person on the face of this planet will benefit, regardless of how it may appear in the moment.

> Until deep desires are touched and released,
> a life can do nothing but stagnate.

Principle #3 Wants must rise above society's judgments

To the degree we continue to seek approval outside of ourselves, to put greater stock in what others think of us than in our own desires, we deny our divinity and view ourselves as limited human beings.

For us to release the shame of Wanting, it's important we understand the benefits which accrue to others—not just to ourselves—when Wants are fulfilled and how to walk out of that ill-placed guilt of putting ourselves before others.

We cannot deny ourselves without denying others. If we deny ourselves some deep desire in order to please others, we're imposing our own guilt on those persons by claiming we are doing it for them. That puts us in the low-frequency position of being spiritually superior, of knowing what is best for all souls.

Our natural flow of consciousness is toward the Light, but the only way to accomplish that is to remove ourselves from the low frequencies of social consciousness. As we learn to engage the higher frequencies of desire, we soon see that in choosing this freedom for ourselves, we are offering it to others by example, by love of Self, by showing that choice is a divine right and power unto itself.

Where does our responsibility lie? To a stranger hurt by the wayside, we have a responsibility outside of "me." To our children and families, if we hold the love we profess, we have a responsibility to bring the light of empowerment to teach and show the way. So, is wanting selfish? Definitely! And so is divinity. The choice is not always easy, but it is most assuredly necessary if one is to reach out of social-consciousness limitations. This brings us to what this entire Tenet is about:

Law of Attraction
Step #2: Identify What We *Do* Want

We can identify all our Wants, but then comes the test. Can we step out of our unworthiness, our shame, our guilt, and everything else having to do with the social-consciousness thinking of "Oh dear, what will they think," and go for it?

Accepting our right to want, and then *allowing* ourselves to want is the biggest test we shall ever face on this journey. Bottom line: This is a test we *must* pass if empowerment is to remain our deepest desire.

> A desire that is within you that is not laced with doubt, is divine. A desire that is within you that is laced with doubt, is yearning.

Is It or Ain't It Exercise

If we can learn to spot how we're holding ourselves back, we'll have a leg up to breaking that habit forever.

The purpose of this exercise is to distinguish a Closed Valve Want from an Open Valve Want. Closed Valve Wants are "safe," and socially acceptable. They won't rock any boats or make us feel guilty. They're also "little" Wants, the kind that won't hurt too much if they don't happen. Open Valve Wants, on the other hand, are straight from our God-self. They challenge our divinity by forcing us into the Light, into a high frequency of joy and excitement and adventure and fun and Life! To reel them in, we must stay above social-consciousness frequencies, out of doubt and guilt and self-consciousness, or they will never happen. Pick any Wants you have already listed, or find new ones. The point here is to learn which is which. One kind of Want comes from our limited, even fearful human self. The other comes from our God-self, forming our empowerment.

My most notable Closed Valve (safe) Wants 😐	My most notable Open Valve (selfish) Wants 🙂

> Our work is to dream things into being, but first we must know what our dreams are.

Principle #4 In order for Wants to manifest, they must *feeeeel* good as we think of them

There are three kinds of Wants:

Real Wants

These are the easiest. Just flip a Don't Want over, and turn it into a Want. Real Wants are what you did in the last chapter. "I don't want to go to Grandma's house for the holidays. Instead I want..." "I don't want to make dinner for everybody tonight. Instead I want..."

Negative Wants

These are the tough ones we'll be looking at now. Negative Wants are really Don't Wants in disguise. You may *say* you want one thing, but your focus (and therefore your vibration) is on what you do *not* want to have or to happen. These can only be recognized by how they make you feel. In other words, you can be saying one thing, but vibrating another.

Rightful Wants

This is what we came here to learn. While they're not tricky, as Negative Wants are, they are frankly the most difficult until we can get past our guilt at wanting. No matter what religions say about giving being so much better than receiving, no matter what parents taught us about wanting being selfish, no matter what friends or family or the world says, "Rightful Wanting" is our purpose here, our mission, our assignment.

> When we focus on the *lack* of what we
> have, lack is precisely what we get.

Negative Wants

o always feel yucky, because our focus is on what we don't
  want

o never get us excited and are never fun

o always manifest more of what we don't want

o are a focus (and vibration) opposite of what we truly
  want

o are always contradictory

o are never high frequency

o are always done with a closed valve

o never give us a charge or make us happy

> Find the feeling place of where you'd rather
> be, what you'd rather have, how you'd rather
> act. It is no more complicated than that.

"I want it, *but . . .*" Exercise

This is the first bullet with which we shoot ourselves in the foot, the "yeah-buts." "I want it, but I doubt . . ." "I want it, but it'll never . . ."

Fill in the pie slice opposite a Want statement with your most corresponding "Yeah-but" statements that you're really feeling but not voicing. "I want this, but…" is our habit of saying one thing, but feeling, vibrating, and attracting just the opposite. So fill in what might be doubts, fears, or skepticism.

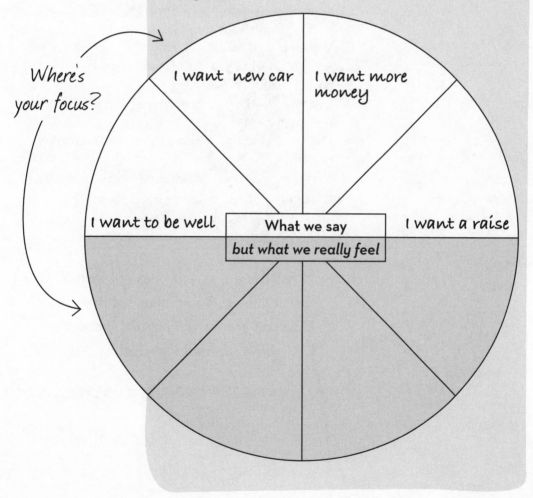

Where's your focus?

I want new car

I want more money

I want to be well

What we say
but what we really feel

I want a raise

> Whatever we're feeling/vibrating,
> the universe is delivering.

 ## Discuss and/or Journal

1. What do the top statements feel like to you? Needy? In lack? Hopeless? Impossible? Negative? Yucky? *Explain!!!*
2. How do your bottom statements feel? The same? Worse? Explain.
3. Where is your focus in the top half—on what you *have*, or on what you *don't have*? Where was it in the bottom half? The same?
4. Can you feel the negative longing and yearning in both statements?
5. Did you feel like your valve was open or closed on both sides?
6. Was there any joy in statements on either side? Explain.

> What you are saying does not matter.
> What you are doing does not matter.
> How you are *feeeeeling*, and therefore
> flowing, is all that matters.

"I want it, *but...*" Exercise Expanded

Contradictory energies cancel out what we want, and an "I want it, *but...*" is definitely contradictory. We're pulsing, vibrating, flowing out energy that is the exact opposite of what we desire, as a result of how we really *feeeeel* about what we're saying.

To bring home the point even more clearly of how we shoot ourselves in the foot, take eleven of your Wants from any of the previous pages and relist them in the left column on this page. Do that first before going on. Now, taking one Want at a time, fill in what you really, truly feel about it. Be honest with yourself. Take time and feeeel *your answer.*

What I *say* I want	But how I'm really *feeling* about it

Unrecognized Contradictions Exercise

The sneakiest way we shoot ourselves in the foot with our Wants is by making statements of blatant contradiction, forever canceling out the positive flow with negative flow.

To highlight how we are constantly doing this, create a contradictory statement for each of these Wants. (Try not to use "Buts;" we've already done those.) For instance, "I want more money; I'm so tired of the struggle." "I want more money" is pure, positive, open valve energy that is instantly contradicted by the negative, closed valve "I'm so tired of the struggle. "No "buts;" only flat-out contradictions.

We want a larger house	
I'm looking for a better job	
We want to send the kids to college	
I so want that spiritual connection	
I've always wanted to skydive	
I want to get a nice tan	
I really want to pass that exam	
We want more kids soon	
I dream of having my own business	
I'm going to have it, no matter what! (And "it" could be anything!)	

It's gotta *feeeeel* good, or it ain't gonna happen

We could go bananas trying to figure out every moment of every day if we're shooting ourselves in the foot by making contradictory statements or sending out "yeah-but" vibrations. The easy way out is to see how it *feeeeels* when you say it. If it feels uncomfortable, find a way to restate it until it feels like you're holding a little puppy, or until you can feel that valve open up to some degree of joy, or until you can literally feel your vibration change to a higher frequency.

Contradictory energies cancel out what we want; the low-frequency negative cancels out the higher-frequency positive. Play with it. "Oh that doesn't feel good, I'll try it this way. Ah, that's a little better." All this takes is practice in being aware of how you're feeling in any moment or in any given situation. If it feels good, you're connected to your core energy. The rest will take care of itself.

Principle #5   Intention solidifies want and desire

Now that we've got the mechanics down of wanting, it's time to leap from wanting to intention so there can be no possibility of our Want turning into milk toast kind of wishful thinking. So now we're going to take the bull by the horns, and *INTEND* that sucker into being. (Never ever worry about how it could happen. That's up to the universe, not you.)

> **"I INTEND! Yes!!!"**

Can you feel the difference inside you when you say "I *intend*," rather than "I want"? Now there is no mistake, no wishy-washing around, and surely, no "buts," not if it's said and *felt* forcefully. Intending removes all doubt. You *know* you are going to acquire this, someway, somehow. It becomes a given.

So when you're ready to begin in earnest with your Wants, take them out of the tentative and shift them into *Intent!* Now you're making a clear statement. There will be no clouding of your energy. It will be pure, and *very* powerful.

From Want to Intent Exercise

Make yourself feel the power of this exercise. Feel the removal of doubt, and its replacement with assurance. Write down any twelve of your previous Wants (do this first), then repeat each one out loud as an Intent... slowly, deliberately, forcefully, and with great joy. Feel the difference, the excitement, the thrill, the anticipation, the knowing! Never mind the how-tos; that's none of your business!

1.	7.
2.	8.
3.	9.
4.	10.
5.	11.
6.	12.

Intention, strongly placed, leaves no room for anything but joy.

This is just the beginning!

All we've done with this Tenet is find out what a Want is and how it needs to feel before it can happen. In the next Tenet we finally learn techniques for energy flow to bring our Wants about. So settle down; the actual "how-tos" of manifesting are coming up.

Meanwhile, here's a quick recap of the most important thing in our lives we need to relearn in order to step into empowerment. We must learn to exercise our right to create. We are creator gods, so what we feel, we create. That is, after all, what we came here to do.

o Begin to identify your Wants; search for them, find them.

o Turn every Want into an *Intent*.

o Get back into dreaming and dream big!

o Learn the difference between safe and selfish Wants.

o Devise more risky Wants ... and more ... and more.

o Learn to feel you Want to ensure it's not a Don't Want.

o If it doesn't give you joy to think about it, change it around.

o Never mind how it will come about.

o If you can't feel it, forget it.

o Always Want/Intend with an open valve, like *"yessssss!"*

o Expand your horizons every day, and never stop.

o Watch your contradictions.

o Ask for help in overcoming any guilt or shame.

o Get beyond society's judgments.

o Want, dream, intend, desire with all your might; it is what you came here to do.

From core, to dream, to intent

Seat yourself in the chair-of-light at the very center of a huge pyramid of liquid white light. See how the light shimmers, reflecting exquisite dancing colors all about you. This is a pyramid of pure love, the pure positive energy of That Which You Are. As you search to find that still, quiet place within you, ask your body to relax every muscle, beginning with your legs, then abdomen, shoulders, arms, and skull.

> **INSIGHT**
> The joy of the dream summons the energy.

You are now, in this moment, the Totality of All That Is. You are not body or mind, good or bad. You are All. You are Consciousness. You are Mankind. You are the planet. You are the Essence of Life. You are Core Energy. *Feel* what you are! From this place of creation, bring forth a dream, a desire, not too big, not too risky, but greater than totally safe. Bring it into your being as you would bring air into your body.

Feel only the substance of the dream. Let yourself expand that nucleus out to find the spirit of the dream. As you do this, find the passion, the thrill. Savor the delight of living the dream, allowing no thing to obstruct your joy.

Let yourself play in this joy. *Make* yourself play, feel, prance and cavort. *Make* yourself feel the thrill, the fire, the gaiety. Now, from this place of core feeling and joy, shift back to your humanness. Turn on a determination the likes of which you have never felt in your life. Set your course, make up your mind, *intend* that you shall have this thing. Whether it be physical, emotional, mental, or spiritual, you shall have it.

While still within the shimmering lights of the huge pyramid, say to yourself, "I *intend* to have..." Mean it. Say it again. And again. Feel the power of core energy that surges through you. Feel the strength.

Come back now, slowly, but never forget feeling that power. Bring it to yourself every day in the form of an Intent, and watch what happens. "I intend...," "I intend...," "I intend..."

Tenet Seven

We are mastering the art of energy flow

WITH THIS TENET WE

- o learn to "turn on" at will

- o examine Step Three of the Law of Attraction

- o discover exactly what's necessary for manifestation

- o learn how to manufacture energy vortexes for every desire

Principle #1 Manifestation happens with alignment

There is a stream of energy flowing to us at all times. We call it Source energy, or the pure, positive energy of All That Is. We can feel when we're letting it flow in (open valve), and we can feel when we're resisting (closed valve). When we're open to it, we feel positive emotions: happiness, elation, freedom, enthusiasm, passion, love.

If we can learn to apply those emotions directly to our desires, and stay out of the conflicting, dream-busting negative frequencies of "It'll never happen," "Where in the hell is it?" "I don't know how," "I'm being too selfish," we can become miracle-makers. The trick is learning to vibrate in harmony *with* our desire, not against it.

So, once we align our energy (what we're feeling) with the energy of our desires (how that desire makes us feel), the physics of the universe takes over to create ways for that desire to become a reality. Put another way, once you start feeling what it would be like to have your desire, the universe has no choice but to hand it to you on a silver platter, *if* you can stay out of conflicting feelings.

The hardest part of manifesting our Wants is watching how we feel about something we want, *but don't have yet*. Obviously we wouldn't be wanting something if we already had it. So learning to stay out of the feeling place of *not* having it is our biggest challenge. Yes, it *can* be done! Whether it seems possible or not, or if it seems to be taking forever to manifest, *you can still feel good about it, whether you have it or not*. That is aligning the energy, feeling good about it, no matter what. Do that, and it's yours. Now—and for as long as you maintain that alignment—you are the genie.

16-Second Exercise

Since staying out of conflicting negative thoughts and emotions is the single most important aspect of miracle-making, it's important we see how hard it is to hold on to positive thoughts and feelings about our Wants. If you can't hold a positive thought about your Want for sixteen seconds, don't worry about it; that will come soon enough. This exercise is only a beginning.

Take just one of your major—repeat major—Wants, and see if you can hold positive thoughts about it for sixteen seconds. Get into the feeling of having it, or having it happen. For just sixteen seconds, hold on to that desire like it was life itself. Feel the joy, the thrill, the accomplishment. Find a clock with a second hand, and get excited for just sixteen seconds. Repeat this three times, separated by at least a minute between each one. From this exercise, you'll be able to see in the days and weeks ahead how rapidly you're progressing. Jot down how hard it was for you, or how easy. Describe what thoughts came in to dream-bust. Note if there was any difference between the first and third session, or the second and third. In other words, was it easier the last time, or no different? Be as detailed as possible. This page will become a valuable record of your unfolding empowerment.

The Want I've chosen is _____

My first 16 seconds

My next 16 seconds

My third 16 seconds

Principle #2 "Scripting" is our magic genie

Our goal is to flow pure positive energy of any kind of joy to our Want, and we do that by getting into the *feeeeeling* place of what it would be like to have it, which brings us to the third step in the Law of Attraction:

Law of Attraction
Step #3: Get into the feeling place of your Want

The only reason we want things is because of how they'll make us feel. And since it's the feeling that magnetizes, all we have to do is find different ways to pull that feeling up... to wash ourselves in it... and to basically live in it for as long as we possibly can. Once we can do that, we've got it made. There are several ways to push us into that feeling place, and one of the easiest is called "scripting," when you become writer, set designer, head of casting, director, and actor! *(but not the producer!)*

As we settle into writing a script, either in our imagination or on paper, we create a focal point that becomes the vortex for us to build upon. As we juice up our emotions over this Want, and talk about it more and more as if it were a done deal, finished, already here or accomplished, the vortex grows bigger and bigger. Things begin to happen. We get ideas of how to do this thing, or have it, or be it. We meet the "right" people, see an ad that gives us an idea, get a hit to go someplace or do something. We script some more, create new characters, new scenarios. Every day, we script a little bit more, telling ourselves how exciting it's going to be to have this thing that we've already *intended* to have.

You write a new script for any thing, any situation, any happening you want in your life. *Anything!* Big or small, meaningful or inconsequential. You write a new script for relationships, money (we'll discuss those two separately), jobs, a new pair of pants, a different hairdo, all while getting into the feeling place of having it, never the feeling place of doubt or lack. As long as you're feeling good when you're thinking about it, it will eventually happen. The more you script and feel good and get jazzed, excited, and turned on, the sooner it will happen, *providing* you don't sabotage it with doubt. Learn to script and to feel your scripts. Your life will never be the same, for you've become *The Director!*

The Art of Scripting

Scripting is the prolonged act of storytelling about your Want, and making that Want so vividly real in your imagination that you can see/taste/smell/touch/feel it as you either talk or write about it (preferably talk). Scripting is telling yourself a bedtime story, conjuring up such marvelous make-believe that you are living it as you tell it. Scripting is making your story so enticing that not one other thing—like doubt—has room to creep in.

The trick in scripting is to stretch it out, adding new characters when the story gets old, new plays, and new visions to keep your juices flowing. In scripting you work yourself up into a lather to get emotionally jazzed, for in that energy your valve opens wide for much higher frequencies to flow out from you in passionate abandon.

The more emotion you put into your story, and the more excited you get, the stronger the magnetism, and the faster that first vortex will form. Remember, it takes only 16 seconds of pure positive energy to create the initial vortex, that magnetic whirlpool now formed out in time, ready to grow into a whirlwind of unseen power that will ultimately manifest your desire.

Once you get that initial energy center formed, all the little pieces—the events, people, and things needed to make this desire of yours—begin to take shape. But the trick is to get lathered up with excitement and passion (not longing and doubt) in order to get that vortex jump-started.

Then, with each new outpouring of passion, you *add* to the vortex, and add, and add, until everything necessary for its creation starts to be drawn into that power center, that tornado of magnetic energy. Before you know it, you've been pulled right into its center. You and your dream have merged. It has happened. You have caught up with it in time. You and your desire have become one.

Prelude to Three Scripting Exercises

"The 25 List"

At the top of the table, list one Want/Intent/Desire. Then list twenty-five reasons why you want that Want. Those reasons can be emotional, physical, or spiritual, it doesn't matter. What does matter is that you stay in alignment with the joy of your desire, keeping your valve open and your joy high! Get into the spirit, fun, adventure, pleasure, and thrill of having your desire. Then, as you list each reason, allow yourself a few moments to feeeeel that reason, to feeeeel why you'll love it so. Take time to savor each answer, each reason you give.

Example: "I want a cabin on a lake." ("Actually, I intend to have a cabin on a lake.")

1. Take your time, feeling *every* statement, *every* reason.
2. Think of every aspect, every nuance.
3. Don't overlook anything; savor every delicious thought.
4. Don't leave anything out because you think it's impossible.
5. It's okay to include others in your dream, but you must not expect that they will conform. If they want to, you've offered the energy for them to pick up. If not, that's their choice.
6. Please, please *please*, let yourself enjoy this.

continued . . .

7. Don't be afraid of feeling good.
8. Fill in all twenty-five! (You'll be using these in three exercises.)
9. Stay out of "how to"s. *They are not your job!*
10. If you really want it, you can't run out of ideas as to why.
11. Never mind "right or wrong," or what others would think.
12. If you think you're being selfish, you're right! (And it's damn well about time).
13. Allow yourself to feel deserving.

My Want is: _____

My reasons why are:

1.

2.

3.

4.

5.

6.

7.

8.

9.

10.

continued . . .

My Want is: _____

My reasons why are:

11.

12.

13.

14.

15.

16.

17.

18.

19.

20.

21.

22.

23.

24.

25.

Good for you...you made it!

126

First Scripting Exercise: *Snowballing*

In Snowballing, you start with mild emotions, then make yourself build to a heated crescendo of passion and intensity, just like good sex. Now obviously, you don't have to start with mild emotions; that's just the way it usually happens. You need to get your juices flowing, and the way to do that is to just start. That's right, just start!

Pick any Reason Why from your "25 List" and place that number in the first explosion (top left). Then talk it into a meaty sixteen seconds of explanation (why you want to have this, or do this, or be this, etc.), becoming more excited as you describe that particular Reason Why.

You don't have to go in order. Pick another Reason Why, place that number in the next small explosion (moving left to right), and make up a paragraph about it while you feeeeel everything you're saying. Force yourself to feel more jazzed and turned on with each Reason Why. Then pick another Reason Why, placing that number in the next explosion. Keep on going with feelings growing until you've created so many hot sixteen-second segments of very excited energy that your Want has been firmly created in time. Note how you're moving from small explosions (little passion) to huge explosions (big passion!). Be sure to talk about each Reason Why out loud in order to keep pumping up as you go.

I intend to…

Second Scripting Exercise, Part I: *Why, Why, Why?*

Whatever it takes to reach that special feeling of joy, to rise above social consciousness to connect with the God of our being, is more valuable than a mountain of gold.

In case the paragraphs you spoke in just now didn't get your juices running, this exercise surely will. In any kind of scripting, the point is to start from an emotional ground zero and build up such a head of steam that there is nothing else on your mind except the joy of having that desire. Your valve is so wide open, your entity could fall right in. You are so plugged in to the pure, positive energy of universal well-being—the love, the abundance, the euphoria—that it would be impossible for you to have any feeling other than supreme, childlike joy. All we gotta do is get us there!

Take any five of your reasons listed on your "25 List," and with each one, ask yourself "Why?" When you answer that, ask "Why?" again. When you answer that, ask "Why?" again, and again, and again, and again until your entire being is immersed within your desire, until can feel the frequency of your body change. Place check marks for how many times you were able to ask "Why?" of the same Reason. If, at any time after you do this exercise, you find yourself shifting into doubt about your Want, come back and do five more. Finish each with your statement of intent.

My reason #1	My reason #2	My reason #3	My reason #4	My reason #5
				I intend to…

My reason #1	My reason #2	My reason #3	My reason #4	My reason #5
				I intend to…

Second Scripting Exercise, Part II:
Probing—Why/Because/Describe

Now take different desires, ones that have nothing to do with your Want with twenty-five reasons, and do the same thing, only more. Make your Wants diverse—some really big ones and some everyday ones. Your everyday ones will show you how fast this can happen, as your resistance will be much lower.

"I want the car because it will make me happy."
"Why?"
"Because I like the looks of it."
"Why?"
"Because it's sleek and expensive looking."
"So how does that make you feel?"
"Great!"
"Why?"
"It makes me feel confident and in control."
"How?"
"Because when I'm in a car like that, I feel on top of the world, like no one can touch me, like I'm king of the mountain."
"Do you like the feeling?"
"Hell, yes!"
"Why?"

See how many questions you need to create before you find yourself exploding with the thrill of how having that Want will make you feel. Each square is a separate Want. Make a check for each question you ask to see how many checks it takes you to get to the guts of why you want anything—JOY!

Yes, this exercise is similar to the last one, on purpose!

My Want	My Want	My Want
Learning to ride a horse		
✓✓✓✓✓✓ ✓✓✓✓✓		I intend to...

continued . . .

My Want	My Want	My Want
		I intend to...

My Want	My Want	My Want
		I intend to...

Third Scripting Exercise: *Storytelling*

Telling a grand story that will change day-to-day circumstances is nothing more than releasing your imagination and pushing it to your emotional limits.

To tell a story with so much heart that we can feel every nuance of our words is nothing more than the ability to dream out loud without fear of criticism, shame, hopelessness, despair, or even impatience.

In storytelling, you tell yourself a story in the tone and warmth of a bedtime story, playing in the world of make-believe. As you begin telling your story, remember that you are a divine, unlimited entity who is living (for now) the human condition. If an idea, a desire, an aspiration exists in your heart and soul, it is up to you to raise yourself above your existing human frequency and bring that desire about.

continued...

Everything you've done so far in this Playbook has been leading you up to this point of mastery. You can no longer be simply an observer of life or a nonparticipating student. It is time to be The Director! For perhaps the first time in this life, you must reach into the brilliance of your own divinity and apply it in a way that will consciously set you apart from the chains of humanity's fear-based consciousness.

Important Pointers of Storytelling

1. Whatever your story's about, *feel* what it's like to do it, be it, or have it.

2. However you do it, talk about it until you can taste it, smell it, be it, feel it.

3. You cannot paint on another's canvas (change them), but you can offer them the paints and brushes. Describe and feel the way you'd like to see them. They will feel—in spirit—your joyous energy; the rest is up to them.

4. Describe (and feel) the new way you *want* to feel and to react.

5. Do this all day with short stories or long; do it all the time about *everything.*

6. Always put in your joy and delight about any little thing you're scripting.

7. Write a new script about one situation each day, or more often. Change the locale, add new characters, make up a new plot.

8. Never mind how it's going to happen.

You've got to design your world the way you want it to be, because no one can do it for you (and never has!!!). By flowing pure, positive energy to your desires, you become the *conscious* scriptwriter. Learn to create your world on purpose by scripting every imaginable situation the way you want it to be, from your heart and soul.

Storytelling: Method I

Building Stories on Reasons

In the "Building" method, you start with one reason and weave it into a story, adding more and more reasons in your story as you go along to move you closer and closer to that point of sheer joy or deep peace or stunning excitement, to that point of absolute connection with your Inner Being, to that point where your valve is so open with pure, positive energy, you and your entity are one.

Here's an example of how my story would progress feeling-wise: "One of the reasons I've always wanted a cabin on a lake is to be able to get up in the morning, go down to the lake while it's so still and quiet, and the fog has mad a blanket over the water (I make myself see the fog and feel the quiet), and just sit and be. There's no stillness like the stillness beside a lake (I push myself to feel the joy of the stillness), at least not for me. Pretty soon I can smell the fresh coffee (I'm feeling the joy of that aroma), and the fireplace. Oh, I do so love the smell of wood burning in a fireplace when I'm sitting by my lake. It makes me feel so at peace ... and ..."

> **Your turn:** *Taking the Want from your 25 List, begin with your very first reason, turn it into a statement of joy, and then weave your way down to the very end as you incorporate joy, fun, excitement, and open valve feelings into every one of your reasons in your story!*

Storytelling: Method II

Telling a Real Story

Now you're going to take a situation you'd like to change and make up a new story about it, write a new script. You can do this with material things too, of course, but for now we'll stick with situations.

Let's say you and your boss at work are forever at odds with each other. No matter what you offer in the way of ideas, you can't get this dork to agree, or even to say "Thanks, but no thanks." You could leave. But until you work this one out, you'll end up with another just like it. So you write a new script, *feeeeeling* every statement to the core of your being as you go along.

"My boss was a man who was having a tough time, and I wanted to help. So I went into his office and asked if he'd like to join me for lunch. He was so surprised, he said yes. We went out to his favorite Mexican restaurant, found a quiet corner, and I started asking him about his wife and kids. We talked about all sorts of things, and finally I told him I wanted to do everything I could to help him. And I really meant it, because I know he's basically a great guy. Boy, you should have seen him; he was dumbfounded, and pretty soon..."

Your turn again: *Think of a negative condition in your life now, and rewrite it the way you want it to be. Revamp the characters or make new ones. Put entirely new feelings into your story, as well as new feeling into you.*

Group Variations on the "Why" Technique

#1: The 15-Minute Red-Flag "Probing" Game

Before playing this game, have everyone bring some sort of red material like a dish towel, washcloth, or even red paper to the group. These will be your red, closed valve flags to wave at your group dreamers as they trip up vibrationally in their storytelling.

When everyone has something red, have each person in the group take turns picking a Want and describing why that Want is desired. As soon as your dreamer gets started, have the group (randomly) begin to probe him with every kind of question imaginable:

"How would that make you feel?" "Why?"

"Why do you like feeling like that?"

"What does your new car smell like?"
"What's it got inside?" "Why do you like that?"
"Who will you show it to first?" "Why?"
"Who will you take in it first?" "Why?"
"How will that make you feel?" "Why?"

Who, what, why, when, where, what color, what smell, what for, how big, what kind, how many? Describe, describe, describe.

Begin the probing gently, building to a crescendo to force passion. For fifteen minutes, you—as the group—want to push that dreamer to the limit of passion, to the limit of allowing himself to feel things he would never begin to allow himself to feel, even to showing off his new car to his stingy father-in-law or taking his kids for their first ride. But more than anything, you want to push your dreamer into joy and excitement and delight and finally... intent!

Now, here comes the Red Flag part: Every time your dreamer lets any kind of a negative statement slip out during this fifteen-minute period, wave your red flags wildly. Any statement like "Yeah, but..." or "I don't know how..." or "I'll start with a small one" or "When I find a way..." That Red Flag is an incredibly effective means of shocking the dreamer into how small he's thinking, or how limited he's being, or how afraid he is, or unsure, or disbelieving.

#2: The 20-Minute Tycoon Game

The difference between the Tycoon Game and the Probing Game is to push one into expansive, imaginative thinking, *as well as* feeling.

For instance (and this is a true story), one dreamer friend had always wanted a camp to teach spiritual values to youngsters, but had never carried his dream past "someday, when I retire, it sure would be nice... maybe... if...," and had certainly never envisioned his dream to be anything more than one little camp somewhere locally.

The group at the seminar began pushing him to think bigger, dream bigger. Since they found no resistance, they kept going and pushing until pretty soon they were *all* getting steamed up and excited, like a brainstorming session but with their dreamer at the center. They pushed him—still willing and open—into having camps all across the nation ... helped him design the camp structure, the personnel, even the marketing, all without knowing one thing about "corporate camping."

The group was getting as excited as the dreamer; everybody was vibrating "feel-good" energy all over the place; the whole process had not only become contagious, but enormously fun.

That was in October. In February, this young man decided to sell his very successful business, quickly found a buyer, located his first camp, found financing for it, and is now putting together a consortium to take his dream national. True story!

The influence of one person flowing positive energy is tremendous. However, the power of a group flowing positive energy toward a subject multiplies exponentially to the power of ten for each person joining in. So, with even just a few people in a group, you're now talking mind-boggling figures of magnified intensity to form and grow the initial vortexes with each sixteen seconds of pure excitement.

The first dreamer in the group begins by telling about his dream of something he has always wanted to build or create: a venture he's long envisioned, a business he's always wanted to have, a book he's dreamed of writing, a band he's always wanted to form, some undertaking of either a "for-profit" or "not-for-profit" nature that he has sincerely desired to pull together but felt it to be either not possible or way off in some nebulous future.

The dreamer will usually begin rather tentatively and almost always quietly out of some unexplained embarrassment. He must make every attempt to describe his project with all the embellishments he can muster, but the moment he takes a pause, the group must jump right in to prod, provoke, and inspire.

"Have you ever thought of…" "Or how about…" If there is resistance, drop that avenue, and go in another direction. Only expand on a particular idea when it's obvious your dreamer is warming up to it, otherwise you're defeating your purpose of flowing open valve energy to the venture.

When your dreamer slips into an "Oh, that's impossible" attitude, wave your red flags, or just wave your arms as the sign of "WARNING!" A minimum of twenty minutes per dreamer is needed to rev everyone's engines. If it goes longer, let it. Keep it fun, allowing your energies to merge and swell into an excited crescendo of creative innovation. You've now set a monumental force into motion.

Principle #3   If we know it, we can change it!

In this chapter, so far, we've talked only of feeling good—meaning getting our vibrations up and our valve open—when we're intending or experiencing the joy of having a particular Want. Our next step, if we are to become true masters of the art of flowing energy, is learning how to flow that high-frequency "feel-good" God-energy all the time, any time. We already know that on any given day, at any given time, our energy flow is primarily low frequency, and we think that is normal.

So before we learn how to deliberately flip from negative to positive in any given moment, let's take a long, hard look at how many times in a day we thoughtlessly and consistently flow out negative energy. Being aware is half the battle. From there, the job of changing our energy flow is fairly easy.

Negative Thought-Balls

Within every conversation or chitchat, with every adverse reaction we have to news, with all the unpleasant things we discuss with friends or relatives, we put out an unending flow of negative energy.

*Fill this negative thought-ball with **big personal worrisome things** you think about all the time, like money, the kids' safety, college funds, job, etc. Pack it with all the **big major** items you can think of.*

Only PERSONAL things go up there, not big global stuff and not little everyday worries or bothersome things. Just big-time things, even fearful things, the ones you think about so often, you don't even know you're thinking about them. Things you think—or talk—about far more often than you'd like, perhaps even all the time.

*Fill this negative thought-ball with **silly little worries**, pesky little things, slight concerns, trivial doubts, pet peeves, casual annoyances.*

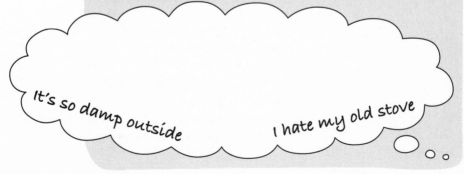

continued . . .

*In this one, put all the **awful global things** you think and talk about, maybe not all the time, but at least sometimes.*

starving kids

wars

*And finally, in this last negative thought-ball, put all the big, ugly, and righteous **nasty moral issues** and **any other negative things** you feel deeply about or talk about with friends and family. Things like government corruption, rain forests, corporate dishonesty, new diseases, prejudices, animal injustices, etc.*

Drunk drivers

IRS dictatorship

 ## Discuss and/or Journal

Apply these questions—and your answers—to each negative thought-ball, taking one at a time. This will clearly demonstrate how endless our negative flow is.

1. Where do you talk about these the most?
2. Where do you think about these the most?
3. With whom do you talk the most about these things?
4. Where do you hear others talking the most about these things?

5. When do you think about these things the most?
6. Do most of your friends talk about these things?
7. Which ones do they talk about the most?
8. How often does your family talk about these things?
9. When?

—*and now the big one*—

10. How does talking or thinking about these things make you feel? Take different subjects, and describe the intensity of feelings that subject gives you.

Here's what's happening with all that "normal" energy flow

First: As we spend the major portion of a day focused negatively, we flow endless streams of low-frequency magnetic energy throughout our planet for others to pick up. Our negative energy—yours and mine—is just as responsible for getting a building blown up downtown as it is for starting a war. Whether we're putting out thoughts of mild disgust or abject hate, it's all negative, all magnetic, and all lethal. We are as responsible as the guy who lit the match.

Second: Any amount of negative energy flowing from us will impact our reality sooner or later. We cannot flow negatively—be it a minor worry or major fear—and expect to get positive results. That's simply against all universal laws of physics. So, if our valve has been unknowingly closed for a lot of years, and we've been "Ain't It Awfuling" everything or been a constant worrier, or complainer, or victim, or excuse-maker, or nagger, our life will reflect the perpetual flow of that low-frequency energy. Finances will be forever bad, relationships will go sour, jobs will not be satisfying, accidents will happen, health will suffer greatly, and above all, moments of happiness will be short-lived.

Third: The more we focus on one thing, either individually or as a planet, the bigger it will grow, for us, and for the planet. So, if we focus on a new disease that has just hit the nightly news and get upset by it, talk about it, stew over it, and complain that nothing is being done about it, or worst of all, become fearful of it, we're just asking for trouble. It will either become a part of our lives, or we'll help the planet grow it into a full-blown plague.

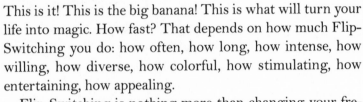

Flow negative out, get negative back,
both personally and worldwide.

Principle #4   "Flip-Switching" is the key!

This is it! This is the big banana! This is what will turn your life into magic. How fast? That depends on how much Flip-Switching you do: how often, how long, how intense, how willing, how diverse, how colorful, how stimulating, how entertaining, how appealing.

Flip-Switching is nothing more than changing your frequency from low to high, but *right now.* It is simple to do, but not easy to remember, because most of the day we feel "normal" and find no need to change. We're not in any kind of negative downer, we're not angry at the world, we're not blaming anybody for anything, we're just being "normal" which means operating consistently in low frequencies. Doing this won't bring you much of anything except your basic, everyday struggle in the form of problems, aches and pains, fender-benders, house break-ins, crappy relationships, and a perpetually short supply of funds. But learn to Flip-Switch, and you've got a whole new world out there.

The key to Flip-Switching is to do it when you feel okay (normal low frequency), not just when your marriage is about to break up, you're going bankrupt, and you just lost your job. It's about performing the very difficult task of feeling good—really good—every single second you can possibly remember to do it. Since it is a near impossibility to have our frequencies high twelve hours a day, then Flip-Switching steps in to become the tool of preference to push us up there. No one will do this for us; it is something we must do consciously, eagerly, and enthusiastically, or it will fizzle.

You can Flip-Switch:

- when you're driving the car
- when you're on the phone
- when you're out for a walk
- when you're going to the john
- when you're grabbing a Danish and coffee
- when you're on the subway
- when you're at a board meeting
- when you're *feeling great* (as opposed to just good), to raise your frequencies from high to higher
- when you're making love
- when you're having a heart-to-heart with the kids
- when you're down, over anything
- when you're frightened, worried, nervous, concerned, edgy, impatient, troubled, vulnerable, uneasy, uptight, depressed, frantic, insecure, sad, doubtful, unsure, ashamed, *or happy!*

All the time.
Any time.
Just DO it.

Flow positive out, get positive back,
both personally and worldwide.

Four Techniques of Turning On with Flip-Switching

Here are the four basic ways to Flip-Switch. Use any or all. When you're down in a deep bummer, use the talking ones. When you're feeling okay, use any or all of the turn-ons. Or vice versa. It doesn't matter. All that matters is that you walk with your valve more open than closed, off automatic, aware of your joy, and flowing buckets of happy, high-frequency source energy to transform your world.

Flow Appreciation

Focus on *anything*, from a piece of dust to a tree to a bug to a street sign, and *flood* that sucker with appreciation. Pour it out until you feel warm fuzzies all over you. Feel the frequency change; feel the adoration, love, respect, and gratitude pour from you for this thing until you feel that familiar happy buzz throughout your body.

Inner Smile Jump Start

This is a good jump-start for any kind of Flip-Switching. Begin by putting a meaningful smile on your face, *not a smirk* but a real, honest smile. It's the kind of smile and feeling you'd have at seeing a mom hold a newborn babe or watching little puppies tumble and play. Feel it grow warmly inside you until you're encased in the glow of this gentle inner smile.

Tough-Talk it Out

This is an out loud, you-to-you talk that is tough, firm, harsh, factual, and grossly unsympathetic. It is tough love at its best as you can tell yourself what a dork you're being for acting this way or feeling that way. Tough talk is often the only way to *feeeeel* yourself out of a crappy situation. It may take five minutes or an hour, but once calmed down, you can then find a way to lighten up.

Tender-Talk it Out

This is good by itself, and great right after Tough Talking. You are talking to yourself, out loud, with the love of a parent toward a little one who just fell off his bike or lost his pet frog. As you feel your tenderness flowing to yourself, feel also the buzz in your body from your raised frequencies. Lovingly and tenderly assure yourself that everything will really be all right. Because it will!

Flowing Appreciation

The closest frequency to that which we are is appreciation.

Take each object listed below, and for a full minute flow out deep appreciation. Keep your focus steady, and try to feel the frequency of your body change as you flood the object with your profound appreciation. Take one at a time, and focus for at least a minute on each. Now go for it! Check off each one as you finish.

- ❏ The nearest wall
- ❏ A book or notebook
- ❏ One of your shoes
- ❏ A light or lampshade
- ❏ A chair
- ❏ The rug or floor
- ❏ Your pen or pencil
- ❏ A watch or piece of jewelry

Those objects were obviously all inside. Next, when you're driving around, do the same thing with oddball objects outside, like street lamps, buses, mailboxes, buildings, etc. In the spaces below, list ten more goofy things you could practice flowing appreciation to while driving your car, only this time you'll make each "flow shot" last only a few seconds. All objects must be outside the car, things you see regularly as you drive. When—and only when—you've felt the shift in frequency take place as you flow energy to each, check it off when you return.

❏ _____ ❏ _____

❏ _____ ❏ _____

❏ _____ ❏ _____

❏ _____ ❏ _____

❏ _____ ❏ _____

Gentle Inner Smile Jump-Start

Just the *act* of smiling changes your vibrations, your brain waves, your metabolism, and your entire body chemistry.

1. Put a real, loving smile on your face. Let yourself glow with it.
2. Notice how good that smile makes you feel—feel the vibrational change.
3. Feel the smile come from the inside, so warm, so tender, so loving.
4. Now let it expand until you can feel a tingling in your head and a whooshing in your solar plexus. Expand it, pump it up, make it bigger, feed it more joy. See how long you can hold the feeling, going longer each time.

Principle #5 Practice is essential

Without practice, nothing in your life will change. High-frequency feelings are too foreign to us to expect that they'll come with ease. Trust me, they won't! But learn to get goofy with silly things to practice on and flow to, and you'll soon be raising your frequencies in an instant, from closed valve to open, from red flags to green, from social-consciousness energy to The-God-You-Are energy.

Whether you're Flip-Switching for a general rise in frequency or flowing out energy to a specific Want, the point is to get those frequencies up. Just watch; the more you do this, the faster things in your life will fall into place: new jobs will come, income will go up, relationships will mend (or do whatever you want them to do), and even health will turn around. Mastering the art of energy flow is not a sometime thing. It takes practice, but the rewards are unimaginable!

The car is an excellent place for Turning On. Do it with Flip-Switching until you can feel that buzz. Hold the high frequency for as long as you can, then make it even bigger, more intense. You may feel a whoosh in your stomach, like being on a roller coaster or it may feel like sexual energy or prickles in your head. Turn on anywhere, everywhere, all day long. Do it until you're so familiar with that new physical feeling of higher energy, it becomes second nature to you. Practice, practice, practice. You have nothing to lose but unhappiness.

Goofy Ways to *Flip-Switch*

1. Talk to your car about how grateful you are that it runs. *FEEEEL it!*
2. Send a flow of deep appreciation to the sun or some rain clouds. (One minute of pure appreciation overrides years of negative flow.)
3. Flow feelings of deep awe toward any resident bug hanging around.
4. Be in love as you walk out the door every morning.
5. Feel wonder as you look at a leaf.
6. Manufacture delight over nothing.
7. Sing love songs to a tree, and mean every word of your songs.
8. Flow profound reverence toward a hamburger.

Now make up ten more.

1. _____
2. _____
3. _____
4. _____
5. _____
6. _____
7. _____
8. _____
9. _____
10. _____

More Practice

Pretend that each of these has just happened—or is happening—to you. Feel your fear/anger/frustration, etc., then decide how you'll Flip-Switch out of it, from a closed to an open valve, and do it!!!

☹ Stuck on the freeway and late for appointment

so I'll Flip-Switch by _____ ☺

☹ Neighbor's dog pooped all over lawn ... again!

so I'll Flip-Switch by _____ ☺

☹ My kids just crashed my computer

so I'll Flip-Switch by _____ ☺

☹ The drought is ruining our crops

so I'll Flip-Switch by _____ ☺

☹ Was just told I'm being sued

so I'll Flip-Switch by _____ ☺

☹ The market is down again

so I'll Flip-Switch by _____ ☺

☹ My spouse was just told he/she has cancer

so I'll Flip-Switch by _____ ☺

☹ I really need a loan, but my credit stinks

so I'll Flip-Switch by _____ ☺

Learn to feel the vibration of happiness.

Changing Vibrations

Before you begin, please put a pen or pencil in your hand. Ask those who walk with you for assistance in this meditation and in experiencing the raised vibrations.

Go inside, center, and feel your Self. Now take in a deep breath through your nose, put a warm smile on your face, hold your breath for a moment, then exhale slowly from your mouth while holding your warm, meaningful smile. Repeat this four more times, turning the warm outward smile into a gentle inner smile as you breathe. Feel your gentleness as you radiate a glow of loving energy. Keep it up, staying there until you can feel your body shift its vibrations, until you can feel that little buzz—so slight, so subtle, but there, nonetheless.

Now, in your mind's eye, find a bird in the sky and bombard it with gratitude for its beauty. Feel it pour out from you.

Now find a telephone pole, and bombard it with appreciation. Feel it pour out from your heart, your head, your whole body.

INSIGHT

As you flow any high vibration of joy, you merge with the God you are.

Now find a tree, and flood it with a love so great, you could weep with your own joy.

Now find a friend, and let flow from you such a high frequency of joy and love as you have never known to be possible.

Now find a mailbox on the street, take careful aim, and shoot it with appreciation. *Feeeeel* the joy of what you're doing, as if that mailbox were about to award you Christhood. (For indeed, with practice, that is precisely what it will do!)

Now find yourself suddenly without funds, and feel your despair. Force yourself to feel deep despondency, fear, gloom. Hold that heavy feeling.

(continued)

Intensify it, make it worse. Now Flip-Switch in appreciation to the pen or pencil in your hand. Flood that little piece of energy with more vibrations of pure appreciation than you ever thought possible.

And now, just sit there and buzz. Feel good, and buzz. Find the joy . . . pump it up . . . feel the tingling in your body . . . bigger . . . more buzzing. Hold it as you come back, keeping it up for as long as you can.

> When you finally understand that you
> can generate that which you have been
> desperately looking for outside of yourself,
> you become the master of your life.

Tenet Eight

We listen, we watch, we trust and allow; then —and only then— do we act

Principle #1 Action is *not* the magic word!

Most folks in America either remember or have heard of the Lone Ranger, the fabled masked man of the West and his faithful Indian friend, Tonto, who, together with their mighty steeds, Silver and Scout, flew into frenzied action week after week on radio, TV, and in the movies to rid the corrupt West of its wicked ways. The problem would occur, and before you knew it, the Lone Ranger was bolting up onto his horse, Silver, and with a mighty *"Hi Ho Silver... Awaaaay,"* went charging off into the sunset to save the day and rescue the hapless victims.

This is what I call the "Hi Ho Silver" Syndrome, flying into action at the drop of a hat to fix, improve, repair, force, push, or coerce in order to effect the outcome we desire. In fact, we're action addicts. We see a condition we don't like, decide what we *don't* want, start trying to bang things into place to fix it with closed valve, disconnected energy, and wonder why nothing works or why we're so tired or why things are getting worse. Still we keep whacking away, because that's how we've been trained. Of course, *we* never win—the problem does.

> Action is *not*
> the main event!

Fix 'em/Bang 'em Exercise

List six very difficult situations (conditions, problems) from your past that you tried to fix or improve before flowing energy to them, either by barging in or plowing doggedly—if not frantically—ahead. Then check off your success factor.

continued . . .

If you had NO success, put a zero under "Low."

My Fixers	High	Med	Low
For example, trying to turn around my floundering flower business		✓	
1.			
2.			
3.			
4.			
5.			
6.			

Now do the same, only with things you started, or tried to get started, such as a new business, or new marriage, or the achievement of some lofty goal. (If you had no success, put a zero under "Low.")

My "I'm-Gonna-Make-This-Happen-Or-Bust"	High	Med	Low
For example, jumping right into marriage after my divorce		✓✓	
1.			
2.			
3.			
4.			
5.			
6.			

Principle #2 It's the flowing of energy that makes things happen—not our actions

In defense of the Lone Ranger and his flying off to fix everything and bang it all into place, he had a good scriptwriter or he never would have caught all those villains. And that's all we need, a new script, and we can catch whatever we want.

Everything we live is about our energy, not about our banging, or "Hi Ho Silvering." So when we plan things from a place of disconnectedness, or out of need as we push against a Don't Want, what are we flowing out? It ain't pure positive Source energy, that's for sure.

Before you embark on any new venture or have an important meeting or go into a new relationship or buy a new house or car or have a baby or go on a trip, you want to pave the way with the energy of how you want it all to turn out. You've got to script it the way you want it to be, or the way will *not* be paved for you and you'll be banging and "Hi Ho Silvering" all over the place.

So script it first. Get into the feeling place of how you want it to be. Flow the energy first, and the universe will organize the "how-tos." Create your own outcome, get into the feeling place of that outcome, and let the universe orchestrate the circumstances and details that will bring it about.

Once you've flowed sufficient energy to your project or circumstance, you create the momentum to form a vortex that will literally suck the action to it. Now your ideas come, things fall into place with incredible ease, and everything is fun rather than work. You begin to take *inspired* action versus *grinding* action—the difference between a success or a flop.

Inspired Action
Actions and ideas come easily, inspired by a higher frequency. Ideas abound, work is fun, everything flows, and life is good!

Grinding Action

Actions are forced, intense, and difficult, if they lack Source energy. They are hard work, boring and tiring, rarely successful.

o *If you flow your energy first,* ideas come, and *actions are inspired.*

o Inspired Action is always fun, always easy. It just flows, one step into the next.

o If what you're doing is difficult, you didn't send your energy ahead first.

o If you've goofed up, you've put Grinding Actions ahead of Source energy.

o *Script it first,* then inspiration will come to tell you what actions to take.

o It's not what you DO that brings you what you get; it's how you are vibrating.

o Scripting—flowing your energy out first—is what brings the inspiration. *Then act.*

> Action without inspiration is tail-chasing

Current Action Exercise

This is not intended to have you berate yourself. Rather it is to show how habitually and "normally" we act, and react, out of low-frequency energy.

The first exercise we did in this chapter showed us what we did in the past. This exercise asks questions to show you what you're doing now, how you are probably attacking your current problems before scripting them with high-frequency energy, which would produce the Inspired Actions to bring about the results you so deeply desire.

continued . . .

MY *BIGGEST* CURRENT PROBLEM

What actions I'm TAKING

What actions I'm PLANNING

How long I've been "acting" (working at it)

Have I been just thinking and not acting? If so, how, and for how long?

How has the problem changed?

ANOTHER CURRENT PROBLEM

What actions I'm TAKING

What actions I'm PLANNING

How long I've been "acting" (working at it)

Have I been just thinking and not acting? If so, how, and for how long?

How has the problem changed?

Fixin' Exercise

When we focus on a negative condition and want to "fix" it, all we're doing is flowing negative energy to it to make it worse than it was before we started messing with it!

List twenty words that are synonymous with "fix." Use the dictionary only as a last resort. We use all sorts of fluffy words to justify and hide the fact that all we're really doing is trying to find ways to fix-fix-fix something we believe to be broken or impaired. (It never, ever is!)

1.	2.	3.	4.
5.	6.	7.	8.
9.	10.	11.	12.
13.	14.	15.	16.
17.	18.	19.	20.

 # Discuss and/or Journal

1. On the previous two pages (do *both!*), how many of your "Actions I'm Taking" or "Actions I'm Planning" would you consider "fixing"?

2. Before going on to discuss or journal, in each of the "Actions I'm Taking" or "Actions I'm Planning" boxes, place the number from the list above that most closely represents what you feel you've been doing. If you can make only one match, fine. If you have twenty, fine. *Be honest.*

3. If you do these two exercises as a group, present some sort of award to the "Fixer of the Month."

4. Taking action before rescripting is fixing. And it's negative! So now, rescript how you *want* the change to happen. Get your valve open, and *feeeel* the revision done.

Instead of fixing it, rescript it!

Now you're flowing excited, happy, high-frequency energy to how you desire your situation to be. Instead of making your problem worse by flying into unproductive action, you're planting the seeds of positive change. And change it will, one way or another. (This time, you might write out your new script, feeling every desired change as you move into the joyful perspective of seeing the changes in place.)

The Master's Creed

To repeat!!!

Never act before you flow!
Always flow before you act!

Instead of trying to beat problems down,
   and fly into frantic action
   and attack
   and lambaste them into place
   and sell more, make more
   and do do do more,
   and fix it, fix it, fix it,
   we learn how to flow our energy, in order to create by ...

Inspired Action
Now ... ideas are all over the place
   everything flows easily (or else it's not Inspired)
   every action produces meaningful results
   no actions are wasted
   there are still challenges, but always quick answers
   you and your Entity are swingin' together
   nothing is too hard or too complicated
   you know how to do it all
   it falls into place, piece by piece, like clockwork
   ... and so ...

Our FIRST job with problems (or "bad" conditions), big or small, . . .
> is to stop focusing on them
> and stop flowing negative energy to them
> no matter how awful they may seem

Our SECOND job with problems
> is to stop flying into go-nowhere action
> stop "Hi Ho Silvering" and stop trying to force things to happen
> stop trying to bang them into place with negative energy

Our MOST IMPORTANT job with problems
> is to see them, but not focus on them
> rescript them the way we'd like the outcome to be
> and flow that feeling out until changes begin

Principle #3   We hear only when we listen

You've identified a problem (a Don't Want). But now, rather than going off half-cocked into the Hi Ho Silver Syndrome and trying to whack everything into place the way you want it, you've rescripted it. You've gotten into the feeling place of how you'd like it to be as if it had already happened.

Your rescripting has changed your vibrations from low, slow negative to high, fast positive. You're plugged in. You've created new corridors of energy flowing into massive vortexes of positive magnetic energy that will begin to materialize your desire. For a while, at least, you're out of social consciousness.

"That's all very nice, now what?"

Now it's "shut up and listen" time while the universe begins to implement the task you've assigned it. If you're listening, this is when the inspiration comes, the lightbulbs, the "ah-ha"s, the fantastic ideas on ways to proceed around your problem—or create your new idea—to bring forth your desire. But you must listen. You must keep your inner ear cocked to hear the coaching from your Inner Being/Expanded Self, as well as from those who walk with you. Or ignore what you get and stay stuck. Listen to what you get and become empowered!

How do you know when an idea is inspired? Check how it makes you feel. If it feels heavy or hard to do, forget it; it's just your old patterning of "gotta fix it, gotta fix it." But if it turns you on even a little, what you're picking up is straight from your higher sources.

And now it's time to keep watch for new happenings that may be the forerunners of the changes to come: things we used to call "coincidences," "lucky breaks," "chance meetings." This is how your new script will unfold, as long as you don't crash it with doubts, "yeah-buts," or impatience.

Perhaps a new idea comes first, in answer to your scripting. Or maybe a forerunner comes first, such as a person, a song on the radio, a detour or a flat tire that takes you someplace special, a call from an old friend, an off-the-wall surprise business opportunity.

Maybe you get a "hit" to go somewhere, do something, call someone. If the thought is accompanied with a little

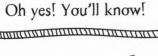

You'll know when to act. Oh yes! You'll know!

tickle of excitement, it's inspired. Do it! Once you've scripted, listen patiently for the inspired ideas. Watch for unusual happenings around you and the odd synchronicities. Script some more and flow some more. Allow it to unfold, and then flow some more. When are you ready to act? You'll know. You will always know.

Discuss and/or Journal

When we're not connected to our Guidance, we have no real sense of what we're doing or where we're going. So we become conformists (better known as sheep). We go along with the crowd, and believe in our limitations.

1. Tell of an inspiration you received or a message you "heard." What were you doing? What did you do about it? What happened?

2. Tell of a time you got a hit to do something or go somewhere, but did *not* do it. Why didn't you follow the hit? What was the outcome then?

3. What does it mean to you to have a "sense of something"? Tell of times you've felt this.

4. What does intuition mean to you?

5. To what degree do you believe you follow your intuition?

6. Can you list ten more words—or combinations of words—we use to describe "inspiration"?

7. Tell of a time when people just suddenly appeared or something "just happened" to help you along— a phone call, a magazine article, etc.

8. Tell of a time when things were very hard to accomplish, i.e., a lawsuit, a divorce, a pay raise. How had you been feeling? The outcome?

9. Tell of a time when everything just fell into place and how you were feeling beforehand.

There's a lot here, but please search your soul for answers! It's important!

TRUST

When I Trusted and Followed My Guidance Exercise

To remind you that yes, even though it may have been accidental, you've followed your Guidance to a great outcome at least once, write in the space below about a time when everything fell easily into place.

1. The thing I'm talking about:	2. The first idea/hit/inspiration I got about it:
3. How that "hit" made me feel when it happened:	4. The amazing things that happened to bring this about:

Principle #4   Trust is the name of the game

"But what if my ideas aren't really inspired? What if they're coming from my need to fix or succeed? How can I trust that what I'm getting is from my Expanded Self or those who walk with me?"

Believing we'll be judged or hurt by society, we do everything in our power not to make mistakes. Yet this is simply social-consciousnss kind of thinking. In reality, there is no such thing as a mistake—just lessons we came here to learn.

Trusting our hunches is not easy; we always want to second-guess ourselves. We want verification that what we're getting is the real McCoy, straight from our Expanded Selves. We want some kind of credential behind our ideas to prove they're the real thing instead of more of our low-frequency fears. We want a set of rules *outside* of ourselves with which to play this game. We are so unsure of ourselves in the arena of trusting our inner Guidance, that when an inspired thought *comes* in, we'll try to intellectualize it or override it in order to feel secure and safe.

The truth is that *the universe doesn't give out Certificates of Authentic Inspiration;* it only gives feelings. If we don't learn to plug in to what feels good, we're going to miss the connection to our infinite intelligence that can give us all the answers to all of our problems.

Your Inner Being/Expanded Self is aware of your every Want, of all you believe, and of all you're working on. Put forth the *intent* that you are going to learn to trust the ideas that give you a twinge of excitement. They're coming in on wings of positive energy. Learn to trust the way you feel. If a million voices are saying one thing and your impulses say another, follow your impulses. Your Inner Being will never let you down.

Did you know that your Guidance system never shuts down? In every moment of every day you are being guided, coached, gently maneuvered, or sometimes hit over the head with a cosmic 2 x 4. When a thought feels good, you're in harmony with your intentions. Follow it through, and watch what happens. Remember, if it feels unpleasant or seems as though it would be difficult to do, it is not Inspired Action. But if it gives you a twinge of excitement, trust it, follow it, *do it!*

> Your Guidance system will never let you down.

TRUST

More on Trust Exercise

The only way we "hear" inspiration is when we're in a high, positive vibration. Then we're matching *us* with *it*. Inspiration is only, and always, of a high vibration (which is why we feel good when we get it).

Take each of the following examples, and jot down your first response. Don't stop to think about what you're going to write! Just write down the first thing that comes to mind. This will help to show how addicted to distrust you are, how much you find "good ideas" hard to believe or trust.

This side is the example of what might come to you as an idea, hunch, gut feeling, or impulse… "out of the blue"…straight from your Guidance.	On this side, write your *first* reaction to that Guidance: What you might do…how you might react. Will you ignore it or not? Be honest!!!
You get a hit to call an old friend who hasn't wanted to talk with you for ten years.	
You get an idea for a fantastic new product that would save people thousands in gas dollars. You've never started a company.	
You're on the freeway late at night. There are very few cars, but you get a hit to exit.	
Your beloved dog is lost, but you have a strong feeling not to advertise or put up signs.	
You get an idea about how to increase your company's profits), but your boss always puts his own name on new ideas.	
You failed English class, but you just got an idea for a terrific book that only you could write.	

Discuss and/or Journal

Our whole goal in this life, our *only* goal, is to learn to live from the inside out. Until we learn to trust our Guidance, we are living from the outside in, disconnected from our Source energy. *That is not what we came here to do!*

> Trust is a feel-good frequency.

1. What does this illustration mean to you?
2. How well do you think you trust?
3. How well do you think other people trust?
4. What do you think it means to "second-guess" yourself?
5. If you've been flowing feel-good energy to a particular Want and you get a hit to do something that seems to have no bearing on obtaining that Want, what would you do? What would you feel?
6. How do you relate this statement with trusting your Guidance: "Mass consciousness will sweep you away and carry you with it."
7. Describe how you can implement trust in this situation: You've just had your feelings hurt by your best friend, and you're reeling from it. But what she said has nothing to do with you, only what she is attracting into HER experience. You just happened to walk into it.
8. Explain "intent without trust is a waste of time."
9. Describe how trust fits into this statement: "When you are moving toward something you want, it's not hard to do, but when you are protecting yourself from something you don't want, it's always hard."
10. Tell about a time you had a strong hunch that you *wish* you'd followed—in other words, a time when you did *not* trust your Guidance.
11. How often do you say NO (or YES) to new or different thoughts coming in?

Principle #5 Synchronicity is the You of you in action

We all want to know if some new thing we're doing is working. "How can we be sure all this energy stuff really works? Aside from actually *getting* our Want, how will we know?"

By the signs, the signs, *the signs;* they become the obvious markers that this is really working. They are the validation we all seek. Once you learn to spot the signs, the game gets to be more exciting and more fun than a week's ticket at Disneyland. And why not? You've just become Merlin the Magician.

Once you've launched your Want on a feel-good wave of energy, two things begin to happen simultaneously:

1. ideas start to light up your head
2. synchronicity begins

We've already talked about the first, about listening and keeping your inner hearing on the default setting, meaning tuned to incoming data. And we've talked about learning to trust what comes in and how to tell if it's an inspired idea from your Expanded Self or just another social-consciousness, fear-based piece of junk from your database of old programming.

But we've not talked a lot about synchronicity. As close as *Webster's* comes to that word is *synchronism*: "The quality of being simultaneous; the chronological arrangement of historical events and personages so as to indicate coincidence." Well, we know there's no such thing as coincidence, but that sure is what synchronicity looks like. Things start to appear. Things start to happen. "Coincidences" abound.

For instance: I've never had to be overly concerned about my weight, but not long ago I started to gain for no apparent reason. I put out a call to the universe, and *Intended* that I be given an answer rather quickly. About a week later, a friend called to tell me about an article she had read in a health magazine on the importance of sunshine and how that related to those of us living in Washington State (we had been through an unusually long winter without sun). It told of how some folks' metabolism slows drastically without sunshine. I immediately got a lamp whose light mimicked the sun's rays and within a month had lost all the weight I had gained without any change in my diet. I knew within minutes of my friend's phone call that the universe was giving me a sign and to listen up. I did. It worked.

A friend of mine put out a Want relating to a new and better job different from his current work, which was selling insurance. Although he liked the insurance industry, he hated selling. But when he started getting brochures about computers, computer programming, and computer repair, he thought the universe had lost its marbles. Then he went to a Super Bowl party and met a guy who designed web pages. "Okay, okay, I'm listening," he said to himself. Sure enough, his new friend was looking for someone who knew the insurance industry to help him design sites for a huge new account he had just gotten from an insurance company conglomerate. My friend took the job. The universe had sent enough kooky signs to get his attention. The rest was easy.

> A sign means your Want is cooking.

HOMEWORK

Pick a *very* simple Want, like wanting to have some different kind of music in the house or some new dishes or glasses some new kind of coffee. Start talking about it with everybody, including yourself. Script it. Feel it. Get into it. Then **start watching** for signs. (How fast the universe responds is how much feel-good juice you've put into it.)

Be patient. Don't get into "where-is-it-ness." Keep scripting for your new "thing," and start watching and listening for signs. A magazine ad? A TV program? A call from a friend? An impulse to go somewhere?

"Here are some funny little things that began happening with my funny little Want."

Number them!

Synchronicity Exercise

The moment you've given your Want sixteen seconds of open valve energy, the universe goes to work. It will bring you clues, signs, glimmers, hints, and suggestions in a myriad of different, sometimes off-the-wall ways. Stay alert!

continued . . .

*On the left, list five of your **Major Wants**. On the right, log all the little things you've gotten that might be a sign the universe is cooking that Want, meaning it's revving up to deliver. No matter how goofy, write them down, by date.*

1.	
2.	
3.	
4.	
5.	

Principle #6 Engage!

You've taken your focus off of your Don't Wants.

You're flowing feel-good energy to your special Want.

You're no longer trying to whack things into place ("Hi Ho Silvering") to make things happen, because you're waiting for inspired ideas.

You're listening to your Inner Being, your core energy.

You're watching for physical signs of things beginning to happen.

You know you're receiving Guidance because inspired ideas are beginning to come to you.

You know that when you go into action now, it will be Inspired Action and evolve with ease. *But the point is you MUST go into action!*

There is never a time when you just sit back and say to yourself, "Well, I've placed my order with the universe. It's out of my hands." No way! Once you begin to get an inkling of how to proceed, or get your first idea, or see someone who suggests something... once things begin to happen, no matter how unrelated they may seem to be, you *must* engage that idea with action.

> Contentment (no action) feels okay, but passion (Inspired Action) feels better.

Remember *Star Trek* Captain Jean-Luc Picard's famous command from the bridge of his starship *Enterprise?* When it was time to move on or set a new course, he'd toss his hand forward with the order "Engage!" You can be having all the good ideas in the world, but you *must* take even the smallest steps every day to implement your idea, or your focus will be elsewhere, and so will your energy.

You must go into action. You must engage!

o no matter how small the engagement (action)
o no matter how little the amount of time
o even if it's just a phone call or two each day
o or a listing of your ideas on paper
o or an actual outline of your project
o or a trip to the car dealer or real estate agent or dog pound or buying some small thing that's related to your idea...

You must do something each day to physically engage your idea.

Engaging (which is Inspired Action) breaks old patterning. Engaging spawns the joy and excitement necessary to magnetize. Engaging will usually create at least sixteen seconds of pure positive energy directly related to your Want. Engaging keeps your mind off of your Don't Want. Engaging in some way, every day, is absolutely mandatory for manifestation!

Daily Action Log

Don't panic, this is only for a couple of weeks. You'd be amazed how easy it is to slough off a day without taking some kind of action on your idea. So, for two weeks (to establish the habit), keep a log of what steps you took each day to further your idea. Unless you take some action on a regular basis, unless you engage your idea regularly, it will never—it can never—come about.

Day & Date	What I did, How I engaged, What action I took	How I felt with it
Mon 6/19	Called Connie to see if she'd like to go in with me on a new business idea	Nervous, but okay

Principle #7 Expect it, then allow the universe to deliver

This is it. This is the fourth and final step in the Law of Attraction:

Step One: *Identify what you don't want*

Step Two: *From that, identify what you do want*

Step Three: *Get into the feeling place of your want*

The Law of Attraction
Step #4: Intend—and allow—it to happen

Now is when you need to cool it, chill out, relax! This is *not* the time to play the "Where is it?" game, better known as sabotage. Neither is this the time to sit and do nothing. You've intended for your Want, and you've flowed excited, open valve, Feel Good energy to it (meaning that you felt *maaaa-velous* while thinking about it). You've even begun some sort of inspired action each day.

Now... cool it, chill out, relax! Take your focus *off* of the fact that your Want hasn't gotten to you yet, nor you to it. Remember, you get what you focus on, so focusing on the absence of your Want will only ensure that absence.

Flip-Switch every moment you find yourself thinking "...but where IS it? Why hasn't it happened yet?" It's that tough business of learning to *allow.* You gotta let the universe do its thing. If your Want hasn't shown up after a while, it all has to do with your resistance, your focus still being on what you don't want, or on your inability to believe this can really happen.

What we think and feel and what we receive are always a vibrational match. Stay focused, flow good feelings, engage, and then remember to *allow.* Your Want will be knocking at your door before you know it.

> Always flow your energy first,
> then engage from inspiration.

 ## Discuss and/or Journal

The following statements are powerballs. If you will truly work with them and make yourself understand what is being said, you will leap forward light years in your ability to manage energy and manifest all of your desires. If you are not openly discussing these statements, then DO write them down. This will more easily push you into unlocking the powerful keys behind each statement.

1. We diligently watch our resistance to receiving.
2. Every moment we feel good in our now, we affect the outcome of the next moment.
3. Intuition is our Guidance in action.
4. If it is not action in joy, it cannot possibly lead to a happy ending.
5. Any action taken from a place of lack is always counterproductive.
6. If the action doesn't feel good, stop it.
7. The more feeling we flow to prepare the way for our actions, the smoother and more fruitful the results will be.
8. We learn to observe by feeling, not by brains.
9. Our Guidance system is about vibration.
10. Listening daily will evaporate our blocks.
11. When we are talking about what we don't want, we are disconnected from our core energy.
12. We will always get whatever we need to support our beliefs, good or bad.
13. What we feel and what we receive are always a vibrational match.

14. Creation comes from feeling, not from thinking, and not from trying to pound things into place.
15. We cannot live something that we are not vibrating.
16. When we are allowing, we and our core energy are one.
17. When we're not sensitive to our feelings, we shut down our Guidance.
18. The more we flow appreciation, we not only connect with our core energy, we connect with everyone and everything in vibrational harmony.
19. Slow manifestation comes from focusing on unwanted conditions.

The universe doesn't take you at your word; the universe takes you at your vibration. All things are created through the flowing of energy.

"Breaking the Cycle"

This meditation is designed to help break addiction to failure. Because we perceive failure to be a reality, and because we desire to see some powerful results of our energy-flowing efforts, this meditation will help pave the way. Do this meditation *only* if you are ready to become a deliberate creator.

Connect with your Inner Being. Ask for assistance. Ask that you be shown from this day forward any signs that you're still addicted to failure, no matter how slight.

And now, climb the sparkling golden ladder that is in front of you, knowing that you are quite safe. Climb very slowly and deliberately, stopping at each rung to feel the change in energy as you go higher . . . and higher. Feel the change. Feel your connection deepen to that which you truly are. Allow yourself to feel your sense of worthiness expand with each step you take.

At the eighth rung, you step off onto a platform of shimmering lavender. Across the way, perhaps 100 yards or so, you see a door. Allow your Inner Being to show you if the door is pure light or pure darkness, knowing that neither is right or wrong, only the experience your Inner Being wishes you to have. There is no solid structure around the door, only clouds of no color. You are bid to cross the lavender platform and enter the door, for this is the door of addiction to failure. Take your time to enter. When you do, leave the door open.

> **INSIGHT**
> We are always pulled by the draw of our own creations.

Inside is total void, blackness, nothingness. You are surrounded by old beliefs, uncertainty, unworthiness, and fear. This is not a comfortable place to be, but you stay, waiting for what is to come.

Then slowly, in front of you, another door appears, glowing with your own divinity, your own brilliance. This is a door of your own making. You are bid to go through this door, but first, reach behind you and close forever the door through which you entered. Close it tightly, firmly, permanently. Now go forward with sureness into the blazing light; go through your new door, the door of freedom from failure. You have walked out of old beliefs. You can never be the same.

Tenet Nine

We acknowledge that well-being abounds

WITH THIS TENET WE LEARN

o health is *only* about energy

o open valves equal safety and good health

o social issues are the result of energy flow

o well-being is the natural state of all things

Principle #1   Well-being is a universal principle

It's hard to grasp that our natural state is well-being, or that we have no reason to be anything but safe and healthy all the time, and that we have no reason to fear cancer or accidents or earthquakes or floods. But it's true. Our natural state is well-being.

Poor health, lack of financial security, job instability, acts of nature, earth shortages, prejudices, these are all the result of how we—and everyone else—have been flowing energy. All of these things—and much, much more—will continue to exist on this planet, but they will only touch those whose valves are closed.

We are either allowing the well-being that abounds on this planet and throughout this universe, or we are not. If we were allowing it in with open valve focus, we would be totally secure, healthy, and prosperous. We may get fired from a job, only to find a better one. We may be brushing up against a tornado, but we'll be fine. We may get a mild cold (from a slightly closed valve), but we won' t get the three-week flu. We may be in a car accident, but we won't be hurt. With our valve more open than closed, with our focus off of our Don't Wants and on our Wants, life turns into a platter of abundant well-being.

With a valve that is more open than closed each day, you won't be mugged (you'll take another route). You won't be killed in a plane crash (you'll miss the flight). You won't be discriminated against, because you no longer are flowing out that negative vibration.

Well-being has nothing to do with contrast. We will always have contrast (likes and don't likes), but well-being is the only thing the universe has to offer. Block it out with negative flow, and we experience the lack of it—big time!

The What-If Exercise

This exercise may seem like it belongs in kindergarten, and that is exactly its point, to show in the simplest of terms the devastating potential of negative energy flow. Negative flow cannot possibly bring about a positive outcome. Deliberate creation is never more complicated than that.

Negative flow equals negative outcome. *Given the circumstances on the left side, note down on the right side what a likely outcome might be.*

In a bad mood, Sam went out to split wood, but his intent was not to feel better.	*He split open a finger.*
Gary was a nasty guy. After a party one night, he was driving too fast on the freeway.	
Nancy hated her job and complained constantly to everyone about her boss.	
Mary knew she could never get ahead because she was a woman.	
Terrified of being mugged on the streets, Jackie's purse was loaded with weapons.	
Moe always looked down on everybody. One day, he went for a medical checkup.	
Sally was charming on the outside, but bitter on the inside. One day her best friend...	
Sue Ann, a housewife, felt trapped and mad at the world. While she was vacuuming...	
Patty deeply regretted her last marriage. When she married again, she...	
Fearing a break-in, Jim loaded the house down with high-tech alarms, but...	
George was afraid he'd be in bankruptcy if something didn't happen soon, so...	

The Well-Being Abounds Exercise

Be careful with this one, because we're starting off with what we would perceive to be negative events. But we're saying that even though the conditions are unwanted (Don't Wants), the outcome is responding to and is the result of one's *predominately* positive vibrations. In other words, bad situation or not, the "flow-er" maintains an open valve.

Negative event, but positive outcome. *The folks on the left have been working diligently at changing their vibrations from negative to positive, with valves now more open than closed. Note a possible outcome.*

Bill's entire department is being closed, due to corporate downsizing.	
Tammy's car careens out of control on the black ice. The cliff is dead ahead.	
The firm never hires the handicapped. Tom is a handicapped engineer, and he applies.	
Dolly mistakenly leaves out a kitchen knife where her two-year-old can reach it.	
A robber comes to the Smiths' home. He starts to go in: once, twice, three times.	
Jacob and his wife are horseback riding—fast. Jake's horse trips and has a bad spill.	
Julie, who can't fly, is in a two-seater plane when her pilot has a heart attack.	
Chris just told his nasty boss in no uncertain terms what he thought of him.	
The evening TV just reported the deaths of two local children from a strange bacteria.	

Discuss and/or Journal

1. Even though the two previous exercises were elemental, what did you gain from them? First, the exercise on page 175. Next, the exercise on page 176.

2. How do you equate these exercises to well-being? In other words, what does well-being mean to you now?

3. What do these statements mean to you:

"You can't always feel good about conditions, but if you focus on them, you're eventually going to achieve vibrational harmony with them."

"When you feel good, you're allowing good experiences. When you feel bad, you're allowing bad experiences."

"The trick is to look at trouble, and keep our valve open."

"You cannot be connected to well-being, and flowing well-being, without having well-being."

"Nothing comes to us that does not match our vibration."

"Your physical proximity to harm and your vibrational proximity are two different things."

"The universe has contrast, but does not have negative energy. Only physicality has negative energy."

"You are not a receiver of bad or good. You are an *attractor.*"

"Well-being is what we are."

> The positive energy of well-being cannot attract its opposite.

Well-being surrounds us, because that is the dominant vibration of the universe. Sure, wars are going on, folks are dying in earthquakes, murders happen, gangs create violence and fear. But how about your neighborhood? Aren't most folks pretty well off, perhaps even moderately happy? Don't most have fairly decent jobs and fairly successful marriages with fairly healthy kids?

So why do apparently good people, who seem so nice and so kind, get cancer or get killed in a freak bus accident or get mugged on the way home? For the answer to these questions, we have only to look at these folks' past to find the strain of negativity—of *some* kind. Perhaps it was inferiority or guilt or regret or shame or envy or worry. Or perhaps they were just classic victims. One way or another, it was their flow of energy that took them out of the flow of well-being.

Well-being is our right. Safety, abundance, security, freedom of choice: these are our rights by virtue of our existence and by virtue of the fact that beneath our physical personas, the well-being of our Inner Being (core energy) is very much alive and well. We have only to merge the two (physical persona and core energy), and we shall have a most exquisite heaven here on earth, as it was intended.

> We are conduits of Life Force energy, meaning WELL-BEING!

Some Major Misconceptions People Have Exercise

The earth is in danger	Cities are unsafe	Flu is rampant	Accidents happen

How many other commonly held negative beliefs can you name that fly in the face of well-being?

Ain't it awful?

Principle #2   Safety is an open valve

Yes, this is like beating a dead horse. How many different times and in how many different ways can it be said that as long as we are flowing predominately positive energy, we'll be safe, protected, taken care of. How? By vibration! So allow me—just this once—to beat a dead horse to drive the point home once and for all, that if you're flowing more *positive* energy than negative, more *positive* energy than flatlining, more *positive* energy than ignoring your energy flow altogether, *well-being will surround you!* It must, for this law is the physics of the universe and our planet: Like attracts like! Everything that comes to you is a match. Everything that avoids you (such as robbers, muggers, drunk drivers) does so because you are now vibrating a different frequency. *Whew!* Okay?

We *cannot* attract negatively when we are flowing positively. There is only one way we clock well-being: *by not flowing positive energy.* Period. Vibrationally, it is impossible to attract anything—*anything*—that is not in harmony with whatever we are sending out on electromagnetic airwaves. The world does not project good or evil, right or wrong, only negative vibrations and positive vibrations. If you want only the "good stuff," *change your vibrations.*

The Beating A Dead Horse Exercise or, My *Old* Solutions

Should we stop protecting ourselves? No. Should we stop locking our doors or carrying mace or taking karate? No. Should we stop taking out earthquake insurance or reduce our fire insurance premiums? No! All of that would be dumb—for right now. Later, maybe, but not for a while, until the hang of this new vibration becomes so ingrained in us, we simply know we are okay and will always be okay. Meanwhile, if a guard dog will help us relax into well-being, great! If new locks will help us relax into well-being, terrific. Whatever it takes.

So this exercise is not to suggest we stop protecting ourselves. It is simply to show how perpetually we focus on our own personal lack of well-being and on what we fear, which, in turn, prevents our desired abundance and well-being from happening.

My Fear or Concern	My Old (or Present) Solution
Can't pay bills.	Work two jobs.

Principle #3 All is quite well on Earth

"Oh yeah? Prove it! We have wars, and horrible atrocities, and ugly new viruses, and rain forests being cut down, and species evaporating, and kids being shot in schools. All is well? That's not what I'd call it."

The sun comes up every day, the moon regulates the earth's rhythms, seeds grow into food, living creatures provide sustenance, waters flows endlessly, our hearts beat, our lungs take in air. "Yeah, but... what about all that other awful stuff going on?" Remember, our planet is *about* contrast, so those kinds of things are always going to exist until mankind becomes a different species (which is happening). For now, suffice it to say that it's not about the economy or overpopulation or the rain forests or the corrupt government. It's about us and how open or closed our valves are at any given time as we listen or read or talk about all the "ain't it awfuls."

Closed valves will harm Mother Earth, yes, but not kill her. Closed valves will produce underground atomic testing and endangered species, but Mother Earth will survive because there are enough people on this planet who see nothing but planetary abundance and flow only appreciation to her for simply being.

Earth's energy is increasing, meaning her frequency is increasing. The more it increases, the greater the separation of frequencies will be for those who are not connected to their core energy. These folks will have a very hard time, causing wars to increase and natural and man-made disasters to run rampant.

Yes, our earth is going through a monumental change. If we do not change with her by matching our frequencies to hers, we will experience the results as highly negative events. If we do change with her and keep our vibrations ever rising, we will never be in harm's way.

The end of the world? Nonsense! Armageddon? For some, perhaps. As you watch events transpire around the world, flow your love to those affected, not sorrow or compassion, for that will simply disempower those to whom you are flowing. Then reach within to find and flow unending gratitude to Mother Earth for her abundance. As unpleasant events befall others, flow the feeling of well-being to them, the feeling of safety, the feeling that everything is going to be okay. That will provide a service to the people involved and will ultimately uplift millions more not even affected by the devastation.

Appreciate this planet, and you will make a difference. Decry those who dishonor her, and you will add to the consciousness of mass destruction, not to mention your own. Remember, the well-being you seek is nothing but the matching of vibrations with who you really are: love, security, abundance, and joy.

Hard-Core Kindergarten

Yes, this is elemental to the point of overkill. But please, please *do* this exercise. Press yourself to find the well-being and abundance that reigns supreme on this precious planet. Doing that will help you relax into your own well-being and absolute security.

Go sit under a tree or by the water or on top of your favorite hill or at a window overlooking the city's skyline. Find your place, become one with this planet, and list all the ways you know Mother Earth offers us profuse well-being. We have but to ask for it and her abundance will be ours.

Principle #4   Shut out Life Force, and you shut out health

Illness exists for only one reason: Whoever is ill has been more negatively focused than positively focused during their lifetime.

Physical problems are the result of various degrees of negative energy flow that have built up over many years. Illness has nothing to do with someone being good or bad, rich or poor. It has only to do with negative energy.

Rich men and women whose negative focus is somewhere other than on lack (where most of the rest of us place our focus) will often die of excruciating illnesses from lifetimes of distrust or anger or misdirected power.

Illness has nothing to do with genetics, except when mixed with negative energy. In other words, just because every other generation in a family is due to contract a certain illness does not mandate that it be so.

Finally, negative energy is the direct opposite of our true body energy. Like anything that lives, the body requires sustenance, but not just in its physical form. The body's cells require being bathed in that high-frequency Life Force energy to live. Squeeze that energy down to mere survival level (it is never shut down completely), and cells weaken and die, unable to reproduce without an abundant supply. Now the body can no longer sustain healthy physical life.

Is illness reversible? Yes, with iron-like focus on Wants, rather than on the illness. Is illness, in all forms, preventable? Yes, if frequencies change rapidly. The bottom line is that negative energy is not in harmony with the body. Feed the body only that, or mostly that, and it cannot possibly maintain a state of health. And remember, "negative" means anything from mild worry to guilt to unworthiness or any of a hundred other emotions stemming from fear.

Discuss and/or Journal

(You will find a considerable amount of material on the frequency of illness, along with exercises to restore health, in *Excuse Me, Your Life is Waiting.*)

1. What happens the moment a doctor gives a diagnosis?
2. Why might a person who is currently healthy, yet heavily into financial lack, be headed for illness?
3. Of the people you know who are severely ill, how many would you say are sublimely happy individuals?
4. As long as someone is thinking "I'm going to fight this thing," where is their focus, and what is likely to happen?
5. What does it mean: "Don't say No to the illness; instead say Yes to Life"?

Principle #5 Everything is a co-creation

We magnetize to us the same frequency that we are vibrating. Getting clobbered on the freeway is an example of two "likes" coming together—head on. The person who gets beaten up has been just as unhappy as the person doing the beating or mugging or robbing. The kill-er is drawn to the same frequency as the kill-ee, and vice versa.

People who die in plane crashes have been drawn to the plane with their similar low frequencies *(that you'd never suspect!)* that will literally realign the plane's mechanics to cause malfunction. Those who do not die in a crash have lived with their valves more open than those who do.

Someone has only to match you in frequency, and the attraction begins. And that attraction will keep on and on until the one doing the attracting gets so tired and so bogged down from a life of negative energies, he will either check out by accident or illness. But now, speaking of cocreations and well-being, let's look at:

Relationships—the supposedly together kind

The single greatest cause of relationship breakup is one's incessant attention to disagreeable conditions, no matter how apparently insignificant those conditions may appear to be. If it's a negative focus, it's a negative focus. Period. Like everything we get in life, from accidents to wealth, it is never about what we do-do-do that equals what we get. Nor is it ever about what the other guy is doing (or not doing) that equals what we get. It is only about our *own* energy flow.

If you want to change the condition of your relationship to one of well-being, you've got to change your vibrations, get your bloody focus off the other's guy's closed valve, and pay attention to your own. Here's how it works:

o If you've got something on your mind, or something is bothering you, open your valve, speak up, and then forget it.

o If you've had more than one relationship that has had the same so-called problem to it, better check out where your focus has been before moving on, otherwise you'll be into the same muck once again.

o Whether or not your partner is a jerk, if something irritates you, you're causing more of it. Remember, *we get what we focus on*. If your focus is on a Don't Want, that's the script you're writing—and attracting.

o If you'd like someone to change, open your own valve first and write a new script. Then, either your partner will pick up the energy and decide to change, or you'll be changing partners. But most of all...

...if it bugs you, get over it!

The "I'm Becoming Aware of All the Silly Things That Bug Me" Exercise

Unless we're cutting off well-being through negative focus, well-being is the way it is. But no matter how insignificant it may seem, if we're focused on something that bugs us, two things are certain: 1) it—or something like it—will get bigger, and 2) well-being will never, ever be present.

The point is not to try to like everything; that would be contrary to why we came here. The point is, however, to change our attitude about those things we don't like so they'll become no-things in our experience, and we'll finally stop attracting any more of what we don't want. In this exercise, put down as many small, pesky little things as you can that bug you about these categories. Remember, everything is a relationship of some sort.

What bugs me about my significant other is:
What bugs me about my _____ is: (Neighbors? Friends? Family? Coworkers?)
What bugs me about my _____ is: (Other relatives? Bosses? Teachers?)
What bugs me about _____ is: (Freeway drivers? Pets? Customers?)
What bugs me about _____ is: (Traveling? Restaurants? Commuting?)

Principle #6   In order to be *for* something, we do not have to be against something else

Civil issues, social issues, global issues, moral issues: if well-being abounds, why is there so much pain in the world? Why do we see so much suffering and wars and lack of respect for life?

The table on the next page lists a few of the major issues of the day—some planetary, others more localized—along with their most common causes, highly abbreviated. These are offered here simply to bring attention to some of the many things we so sincerely dislike or would like to change or would like to get rid of so that well-being could truly abound. But would it?

No. Although well-being is the predominate frequency of every being in this or any other reality, and of your Core Entity, your Source, and all Life Force, on this planet it will never completely take over for one simple reason: Physicality is a training ground for discernment—what we came here to learn.

However, even though we may never completely stop all negative events, we can most assuredly help to lessen them, turn them around, make them less devastating, and yes, in some instances, eradicate them altogether so that greater and greater well-being can abound. We do this by changing the way we think about world events or moral issues, which means that ultimately we will change the way we *feel*. Not only will such changes affect the event for the better, but will strongly influence our own personal lives as well.

We must stop—we *must* stop—our interminable negative focus on what we deem to be negative events or circumstances. "Isn't it terrible?!" "What will we do?!" "They've always been against us!" "What they're doing is awful!" "How very sad." Those kinds of vibrations flowing from us will do nothing but make bad situations worse. Then, as we compound our own negative energy and focus with millions of others who are being so negatively impacted by our

> Well-being is the natural state of All That Is, including you, the universe, the planet, and all upon her.

> Our focus on what is wrong creates more of the same.

media, "bad" things on this planet have no chance whatso-ever of turning around, improving, or even ceasing.

Our job, then, is to find ways to rethink, and then *re-feeeeel* these events. We can best do that by realizing that every soul on this planet came here to learn *something* and that sometimes those choices seem mindlessly harsh to us. If we will flow quiet joy instead of "Ain't-It-Awfull-ness," allow-ance instead of hatred, gratitude to the planet instead of agony over her plunder, if we will simply make an effort to *feeeeel* differently, we can change the world, not to mention our own lives.

The "Rethink It" Exercise

Some of the events and circumstances we abhor (To better understand why these things happen at all, see *Excuse Me, Your Life Is Waiting*, Chapter 11)	Possible new ways we might think and feel about them now.
Moral Issues Dolphin killings, global warming, animal rights, endangered species, atomic bomb testing	
Mass Killings Genocides, holocausts, massacres, bloodbaths, mass torture, war	
Teens Suicides, pregnancies, drugs, guns, car accidents, drug use, dropouts	
Global Terrorism, famine, disease, child slavery, floods, ocean warming, earthquakes	
Prejudices Race, sex, sexual preference, body types and shapes, nationalities, cultures, religion	

Principle #7   Death is a cosmic joke

An untimely death is from a closed valve, from fear or self-hate or guilt or... When self-acceptance and all those good feelings are flowing through you, well-being abounds!

As long as we fear death, we retain a vibration of fear in the body, therefore disallowing our desires. So how do we get over that universal fear? By realizing that we can't kill energy, which is what we are. Death is only of the body, not of our Selves. Death is only a change of frequency, a change of focus, a change of costumes. We simply step from one frequency into another.

This unnatural fear of death is a learned response from people who have desired to control us with that very same fear. But the truth is we don't die, we just disconnect from the disconnection in which we've been living. Then we re-emerge into full nonphysical empowerment. But the point of our being here is to learn to have that same empowerment IN the body, not wait until we're outta here.

Remember, the You of you never quits. It is forever; you can't kill the Life Force you are.

The "We've Always Believed It" Exercise

It's not the cigarette smoke that kills; it's the disallowance of positive energy. It's not the bad heart that kills; it's the lack of joy in one's life.

Inside the skull and bones, list thirteen other ways that we have always considered to be normal, death-causing events or circumstances that come from the old victim "they did it to me," "it wasn't my fault" kind of thinking.

A Few Final Thoughts

Force yourself to look for the well-being that is there, be it in government, the economy, wars, disasters, pestilence, localized massacres, relationships, or even on TV. Look for it, and decide to *find* it! By doing that, not only will you change the planet, you will bring endless buckets of well-being into your own life. Guaranteed.

And so . . .
> Open your own valve no matter what,
> no matter what
> no . . . matter . . . what!!!
> The rest will take care of itself.

We cannot be connected to well-being, and flowing well-being, without *having* well-being, because not one thing comes to us that does not match our vibration.

The bottom line is:
> What we focus on is what we feel.
> What we feel is what we vibrate.
> What we vibrate is what we attract.

When enough of us on this precious piece of real estate begin to get even a small amount of our negative energy turned to positive flow, wars will stop, trees will grow, suicides will be a thing of the past, prejudice will evaporate, natural disasters will all but cease. Like attracts like. That is the way it is.

> Open valves connect us to our core energy, bringing well-being. The more connected we are, the more well-being abounds. *Open your valve!*

I *Am* Well-Being

Close your eyes . . . and take a few moments to relax fully with several deep breaths. When you are ready, visualize yourself at the center of a massive figure eight of liquid white light. Send the bottom of the figure eight down into Mother Earth, looping it around her core. Now make the figure eight top-heavy by looping the upper half far, far up into the universe. Remember, you are the center, so now . . . shine! shine!! shine!!! Intensify both loops from your center and make the light of your figure eight glow with lots of love.

Sit for a moment and *feeeeel* what you are doing. Allow your frequencies to rise. Feel the love you are sending to—and wrapping around—the center of Mother Earth. Feel the love coming back to you from the universe, down the light-lines of your huge loop. Feel that love flowing into you, then flow it out. Feel it. Feel it. Feel it. And now, as you continue to intensify the light, the magnetics, and the love flowing and attracting from both loops, say silently and *feeeeel*, "From this moment on, I intend for well-being to be the dominant vibration of my life.

> **INSIGHT**
> Our natural state is one of well-being.

"From this moment on, I will say *yes* to well-being.

"From this moment on, I will remember that the core of me, my essence, the totality of all that I *am* is security, wellness, freedom, knowing, and well-being.

"From this moment on, I acknowledge that my Source is pure well-being, and *I am my Source.*

"From this moment on, I will do all I am capable of doing to remain in harmony with this greater vibration that *I am.*

(continued)

"And now, from the Light of God that *I am*, I ask all who walk with me, all who teach me, and all who stand by me to assist me in relaxing into the vibration of well-being, and into the absolute knowing that all is truly well. Above all, I ask my God-force to flow within me at all times, and to help me feel the power and the security of that flow. So be it!" Come back slowly, knowing you have changed.

The more energy of love you flow out, the more of it you will become.

Tenet Ten

We live from the Now, not from the Past

Principle #1   The ONLY place we connect with divine power is in the Now

How do we get it? How do we create that special feeling of connectedness with the God of our being, our true Selves, those priceless moments of ecstasy we've all felt at one time or another? And is it really possible to experience a connectedness with our core energy while rushing to catch the 6:58 to work? And even if we can do this, what's the big deal about it? What's wrong with just feeling the way we normally feel?

That nebulous "Now" is more important to us than sunlight or winning the lottery. It is more important—almost—than breathing, because without the high-frequency moments of "Now" we experience all too infrequently (except during sleep) we would cease inhabiting the body. So what is this Now thing?

Every time we raise our frequencies, we move into the Now. Every time we feel appreciation, gratitude, joy, preciousness, love, excitement, etc., we are in the Now. And here's the bottom line: every time we are in the Now, we are in a higher frequency, connected to our core energy, therefore attracting desires.

But the trick here is that we attract *everything* from how we're vibrating in the Now, good or bad, wanted or unwanted. To tackle this confusing dilemma, let's make two different kinds of Nows: one will be the Divine Now, and the other the Normal Now. In the Divine Now, our valves are very, very open. We are in love with life, fully connected to our high-vibrating Source, manifesting well-being and abundance. In the Normal Now, our valves are closed. We are manifesting from our past by either hanging on to old beliefs, or responding to unpleasant conditions in the Now. So let's find out how to get into that Divine Now, and *stay* there!

How conscious are you *now* of your vibrations?

Remember that as we keep on *feeling good* we're forming a vortex of energy so powerful that any energy necessary to create whatever we want is being sucked right into that vortex. And *feeling good* means being in the Divine Now. Our conclusion, then, is rather obvious: Unless our valves are open and we're feeling way-up-there good, we're in the Normal Now, not the Divine Now, and not about to manifest anything close to our desires. As a quick but important refresher, let's identify what *feeling good* really means.

 ## Discuss and/or Journal

How I open my valve when it is very closed:

1. When I see something I don't like, I …
2. When I'm deeply annoyed at someone, or hurt, I …
3. When I feel angry over world events, I …
4. When I'm worried, I …
5. When I don't feel loved, I …
6. When I'm frightened, I …
7. When I want to fix someone, or something, I …
8. When I feel bored or insecure or left out, I …

How I open my valve when it's only a little closed:

1. When I'm not feeling either up or down, I …
2. When I'm at work, and everything is sort of okay, I …
3. When I'm talking with someone, and not feeling much of anything, I …
4. When I get up in the morning, I …
5. When I go to bed at night after an okay day, I …
6. Whenever I catch myself starting to go down, I …

How I *know* my valve is open:

1. I can tell my frequency is high when I feel...
2. I know my valve is open because I...
3. I know when I feel joy because...
4. I can feel it when I flip-switch because...
5. When I can turn my focus from..., I know my valve is open.
6. I can always make my valve open by...

In Which Now? Exercise

All right, now let's use those same understandings to see exactly when we *are* in the Divine Now, when we *are* connected to our core energy, and when we *are* manifesting our desires.

Fill in the right-hand areas with every emotion, state of being, or conscious awareness you can think of that matches a closed, partly closed, or open valve.

I know my valve is pretty well closed when I feel...	Normal Now **Full of doubt**
I know my valve is only half open, or only a little open when I feel...	Normal Now **Nothing**
I'm dang sure my valve is *way* open when I feel...	Divine Now **Real joy**

Principle #2 The universe does not want your resume

"The reason I'm this way is ..."

"I've been this way all my life, but now I'm trying to ..."

"If I could just get rid of that awful trait of mine, I'd ..."

"I'm working on it ... God knows I don't like myself like this, but I'm working on it."

"Will I ever learn to ...?"

Processing, processing, processing. Stop it!

As long as we are processing, it is absolutely impossible to live in joy or pull in our desires, for we are only focused on, and thinking about, and feeling, and therefore *vibrating* all that old, ancient junk. Processing is guaranteed to tie us forever to our past, from which not one of our desires can ever manifest. Not one desire—not ever. *Not ever!*

As long as we're trying to process our stuff, meaning trying to fix ourselves through this endless focus on where we've come from, what happened to us, and all the other long-gone circumstances of our past, we will never—we *can* never—live in the Divine Now of joy.

The universe recreates itself around our pictures of reality. (We always get what we focus on, remember?) If we hold a picture of reality that there's something wrong with us, or that we need to be fixed, the universe has no choice but to recreate what we're feeling and what we're vibrating.

> Stop processing; start living! Stop dissecting; start experiencing!

No one is asking you to deny your past. In fact, as you raise your frequencies, more and more unpleasant feelings are going to pop up, like shame, guilt, fear, and despair. But processing this would take forever, because you would have to process each lifetime separately—*not just this one*—to clear away all the emotional baggage.

So rather than denying or stuffing your past, go ahead and look at it, but without judgment. Look at it, express it, admit it, acknowledge it, accept it, and move on. In other words, let your past become something that is simply a matter of fact. That's all. *Express* your disappointment, your regret, your anger, and then … *let it go!!!* If you don't, you will continue to draw to you the very events that you are still resenting or regretting.

So never mind where you are not; decide where it is you want to go! Never mind how you got to where you are now; decide where it is you want to be! Every moment you spend explaining how you got to wherever you are now you bring that past into your Now and vibrate it. That can never, *ever* make for a Divine Now, with positive energy flow, where you are connected to your core energy with a happy, open valve. So stop processing and start living. Where is your focus? What are you vibrating?

Learning to Marvel

Before we do exercises relating to moving beyond our past, we're going to add a new word and feeling to our bag of tricks for ways to rocket us into the Divine Now.

All things manifest from the Now. And so, to keep us from constantly re-creating our past, our goal is to find the easiest way to Flip-Switch us out of that old focus and into a higher vibration. Learning to "marvel" is a way to do just that. It is a vibration as high as appreciation and often easier to reach.

> The signal you are putting out is giving you the life you are leading.

The "You'd Be Amazed at All the Goofy Things You Marvel At" Exercise

Do this one square at a time! Write down the goofiest thing that is within your line of sight (e.g., birdbath, crack in the wall, paper clip, dead leaf), and make yourself marvel at it for ten seconds. Do this over and over until you can finally feel that sudden—though subtle—change in your frequency, meaning how you are vibrating. Write down your item, then put a "Yes!" when you have successfully felt the marvel of that wondrous, goofy item.

The rug— YES! Fast! WOW!		

The Moving Beyond Exercise

If we could get up in the morning determined to look for things that made us feel good, then when we looked into our past, that's all we'd find. Once we've created the *habit* of feeling good, the past becomes a no-thing, as does our need to process.

Use your new feeling of marvel to do this. Let the feelings of wonder, awe, and respect flood through every cell of your being as you marvel at your toothbrush or coffee cup. Then, instead of processing, Flip-Switch to marveling over something, even your past (especially your past!). Soon your past will be unimportant, because you will be living from the Divine Now. And you will be happy! If you will do this every day for one solid week, you will be flabbergasted at how fast your past becomes unimportant, along with your need to process.

When I got up this morning, I was thinking about…	It made me feel…	So I decided to forget that, and instead, marvel at…	It worked? Or not?

Principle #3 Following our joy is what we came here to learn

My favorite magazine ad of all times, from the General Nutrition Center people, is laid out exactly like so (I have it on my bathroom wall):

> "You are here to get kites stuck in trees.
> You are not here to catch trains and wear dress socks.
> You are here to build things and teach things and jump into lakes.
> You are here to make things better for others, better for yourself.
> You are here to laugh, take naps, and run around the base paths.
> You are here to live well."

There it is. the crux of all we've been working on and toward: being in joy. When we can look into this world and feel joy all the time, meaning some degree of joy in every experience, then we have become a grand Master of energy flow. Our lives will be fantastic. We will be on our way to grand abundance, health, and happiness. All it takes is practice.

The only place we will ever find joy is in the Divine Now where our frequencies have risen above social consciousness. Negative emotion is an absolute deviation from what we really are, yet negative emotion is all we have when we dwell unhappily in the past.

Learn to feel the joy of what is before you rather than the pain of what is past. Health, freedom, joy, and abundance are all the same vibration, so learning to follow our joy seems rather important. The openness or closedness of your valve—how much Life Force you are summoning to place you in a higher frequency—is directly proportional to the joy you feel. Marvel? You're in joy. Appreciate, love, laugh? You're in joy.

When your joy no longer depends on what anybody else thinks of you, or what anyone else does, then you've "got it." When you can allow, even when "they" are not allowing you, then you've got it. All it takes is a little practice.

HOMEWORK:

Making a joy list
Keeping a joy list

The only reason we're starting this homework here is to get you beyond the obvious. This will undoubtedly be one of the most difficult exercises in this book, because most of us have never given more than a passing thought to what gives us joy. Oh sure, there will be the normal things like "going deep-sea fishing," or "taking a long bubble bath," or "watching a beautiful sunset."

But then, after you've put down about ten of the most obvious, ask yourself how often you do those most obvious things. How often do you go deep-sea fishing? Since you usually shower, how often do you take bubble baths? And how often does your locale present you with an outstanding sunset?

Indeed, this will take daily work. You'll probably find yourself jotting some "joys" down on matchbook covers, or napkins, or inside books. Fine. Do that, then transfer them to your main Joy List, wherever you want to keep it. Just make sure it's ongoing. Then, as you find your list growing, the point is to do more—more often—of what's on that list. So here we go: one of the most fantastic exercises the cosmos ever gave us—creating your very own Joy List.

> Ask yourself what makes you happy, and do it. The more moments you spend being happy, the closer you are to being the God-force of all Life.

Your Joy List

List only the most obvious here, then keep this list going somewhere else.

| |
| |
| |
| |

MORE HOMEWORK

Because so many of us feel we can't be in joy without money (an erroneous belief if ever there was one, but let's play along), or that we can't be out of stress without money (again, way off base, but we'll play along), let's implement one of the most powerful money games the cosmos has given us to date.

The "Charging Into Prosperity" Game

First of all, you must decide to do this every single day, or it won't work. Next, you can't just *do* this; you've got to *feeeeel* it every time you make an entry. You're going to be depositing vast sums of money into an imaginary account, but if you can't work up enough enthusiastic pretense to make believe that you are actually doing this, forget it. You're not yet ready to break out of lack. Making each deposit must be like savoring a magnificently delectable piece of cuisine being offered to you by one of the world's finest chefs. You feel the joy, the freedom, the power, the relief, the pure, unabashed gratitude of each deposit you make, and each check you write.

> *Okay, here's how this works, and believe me, it does work. This is extraordinarily powerful stuff if allow yourself to get into the thrill of it.*

1. Get a checkbook to work with (often your bank will have sample checkbooks they no longer use. Ask them, or just use one of your own.)

2. Starting with $1,000 deposit from day one, each day add another $1,000 to the previous day's deposit, like so: $1,000 on the first day, $2,000 on the second day, $3,000 on the third day, etc.

3. When you have deposited sufficient income to purchase your first desired item (from the Intend List

you've made on the next page), you purchase that item by writing a check for it.

4. Place your written checks in an envelope that is in plain view somewhere. In other words, don't just stuff them away to be forgotten.

Item #	Date	Transaction Description	Deposit	Withdrawal	Balance
1	7-6		1,000		1,000
2	7-7		2,000		3,000
3	7-8	New furnace	3,000	5,500	500
4	7-9		4,000		4,500

$66,000,000

Right! If you continue depositing as shown, at the end of one year you will have deposited over $66,000,000. So give that open valve energy some *major* outlets to flow toward.

In the spaces below, begin your Intend List, creating three items in each box, and then continuing your list elsewhere as these fill up. Make time to carefully budget, planning how much each project or item will cost as you stay joyfully, excitedly, and intentfully in the Now (not to mention breaking you into abundance!). Find a balance with your Intent Items... not too big (until you're honestly comfortable with "big"), and surely not too small. Get out of your old beliefs, let yourself feel the thrill of this, and watch the universe respond.

continued . . .

1.	2.	3.
1.	2.	3.
1.	2.	3.
1.	2.	3.
1.	2.	3.

Principle #4   All negative emotions come from the past

Along our path in life we pick up *this* belief and *that* belief, and a few hundred others that don't always make us feel good when we think about them. Sometimes we know what they are. More often than not, we haven't a clue what's stuffed in our subconscious. Without knowing, we find ourselves thinking a particular way and wondering why we're not feeling so hot. It's old, outdated beliefs, old, outdated habits of thinking.

And yet, there are no negative vibrations stored in us, just old patterns of thought, old habits of thinking that, when brought into the Normal Now, make us feel crawly with varying degrees of negative emotions. And we feel that way because those thoughts are in direct contradiction to what we know to be the truth of the Divine Now—meaning, we know the supposed cause of however we're feeling is no longer a truth, just a habit of thought.

We've already done some work on ferreting out old, unwanted beliefs, but this time we're going to take a different approach. We're simply going to override whatever the old thought or feeling is and shoot ourselves right back into our Divine Now where there is no feeling bad over anything, only feeling good over everything. Our point here is to **never mind what the subject is;** *concentrate on how you feel!*

Since our entire physical environment is the materialization of our beliefs, let's just make a decision that no matter how powerful the belief may be (e.g., you gotta work hard to make money, men get better jobs, I'm a product of my past), we're going to override it simply by concentrating on how we feel.

Remember!

o A belief is nothing but a habit of thought. You can always tell you're having one of your habits by how you *feeeeel*.

o Old beliefs will only activate at certain times. But when a block hits, if you can identify it, great. Identify it, own it, then override it with one of the "dos" on the next page.

o Beliefs, whether known or unconsciously stuffed, generate emotion, and emotions generate vibrations.

o Even if we think the belief is too big to ever go away, all we have to do is Flip-Switch into a prolonged "do" each time it comes up. Not only will that override it in that moment, we will eventually cause it to go away forever.

o We are not at the mercy of events that transpired in our childhood unless we believe we are.

> It's so important I feel good that I'm going to behave differently more of the time!

The "I'm Outta the Past for Good" Exercise

When we feel good, we're in the Divine Now, connected to our core energy with open valves and vibrations that are high and positive. When we feel good, we're not sending out negative vibes by stewing over the past or worrying about the future. It would seem, then, that anything we can do to feel good would be a wise move.

This one is ACTION, as opposed to just LISTING.

continued . . .

This is similar to your Joy List, except you are listing things here that are action-oriented for daily life—just nice little things that make you feel snug or satisfied or good about yourself or content and happy. Things that you can do more of on a regular basis. Remember, once you put them down on paper, you will do them more often, thus attaining more of the Divine Now.

It's so important that I feel good, I am going to:

For example: spend more time with this friend or that one; change my magazine subscriptions to ones I really want; find more books I want to read; wear more clothes that make me feel comfortable; stop worrying about the future; stop watching TV shows that bore me.

1.

2.

3.

4.

5.

6.

7.

8.

9.

10.

Living the Power of Now

If you can, find a quiet place in nature where you can bring your focus into the Divine Now by examining a tiny flower for its exquisite expression of symmetry and color, or where you can sit at the base of a great tree, or atop a quiet grassy knoll. If you cannot do this in reality, then take yourself, in your imagination, to a great forest where the birds are singing, the wildlife is all about you, and the sun is streaming down in through the trees. Let yourself feel the power that surrounds you, the serenity, the sureness, the utter Divine Now.

As you begin to feel the power that surrounds you seeping into your being, realize that what you are feeling is simply the power of the Divine Now. The joy you feel as you smell the fresh air is the power of the Divine Now. The peace you feel as the sun soaks into your grateful body is the power of the Divine Now. The happiness you feel with the breeze is the power of the Divine Now. The presence you feel as the water splashes around you is the power of—and unconditional, all-encompassing love of—the Divine Now.

The consciousness of nature accepts you, for it sees you as no different than that which it is: timeless in the Divine Now. Allow your heart to expand and reach out to all that is about you as all that is about you reaches out to you. Feel the presence of Now, a state of purity and knowing. Feel the love that engulfs you . . . from the forest, the shrubs, the animals, and all that is unseen. Feel the peace that exists between you and all Life.

> **INSIGHT**
> Happiness is
> an inside job.

As you have created this precious moment, realize that you too can create all of your moments to come. As you watch the stream tumble to the sea, realize it flows with purpose, as can you. Stay perfectly conscious of everything that is happening to you in this moment, inside and out . . . and the next moment, and the next. Pay attention to *Now*, and you will live tomorrow what you are happily drifting through today. Divine power is yours, in the Divinity of Now.

Tenet Eleven

We stretch our God-consciousness daily

WITH THIS TENET WE LEARN

- o the magic of Desire

- o the magic of decisions

- o that in the asking comes the connection

- o how to empower a sense of greatness about ourselves

Principle #1 — Empowerment is the willingness to forge ahead, no matter the unknown

"God-consciousness." What does that mean? How will it make us feel any different from what we experience as reality today? What good can come of it?

To become the powerful magnet we were intended to be, we must master the art of expanding the force field of our minds in ever-widening concentric rings. We must train the energies of our consciousness to flow outward in infinite circles from the center of our awareness to the periphery of our God-self awareness, and then back to the point of identity within. Then, immersed in the energies of light, life, and love, we take in more and more of the consciousness of our Core, our Source, until the waves are gone and we become one with All That Is.

Our goal is to establish our consciousness as a force field of divine power, bringing within us a divine magnet that will attract more of God, more of good. Once we learn to control that force field with the knowingness of a God incarnate, we unleash unlimited potential to have and to be whatever is our divine Desire.

When we make the decision to become empowered, to enter into the process of transformation (as we have been doing all throughout this Playbook), we soon realize that we can feel our divinity even in the midst of our humanness. We find that we can turn within to our own power and find answers.

Empowerment is learning first to accept, and then to stretch our God-consciousness—our true power, our true nature, our true Selves—daily. Empowerment is not a happening, it is a willingness to become far more than what we have known to date. Empowerment and stretching our God-consciousness are one and the same thing. It is learning to feel—and to be—our divinity.

Discuss and/or Journal

Certain actions, when taken, will greatly empower your Inner Being and your sense of greatness about yourself (though that may still be hard to swallow). One of those actions is to acknowledge whenever some new thing has happened within you, no matter how small or apparently insignificant. These are the "ahas," the new kinds of thoughts, new awarenesses (whether they last or not), and even lack of RE-actions. The more you acknowledge these awarenesses, the faster your own empowerment will be. The importance of this step, of acknowledging your growth, cannot be—*must not be*—glossed over.

> *List and discuss now, and keep a journal of, all the new awarenesses you have had since beginning this program. To refresh your memory, look back over each Tenet and jot down one or two awarenesses from each one. For instance:*

o When did you really find yourself "listening"?

o How often now do you Flip-Switch?

o Can you look at death and destruction on the news now and still feel that all is well?

o Has your view of death changed?

o How do you handle contrast now, as opposed to "back then"?

Now hang on . . . there's a *very* new way of looking at this.

When you decided to embark on this journey, you empowered yourself by beginning to live the life of a warrior. Huh? Oh yes! If you've gotten this far (which is almost to the end of this book, but not the program), then you've already taken on the characteristics of a warrior. Odd as this may sound, until you can feel like a warrior, and are willing to go to any lengths, empowerment will elude you.

This means you must continue to find ways to expand your awareness, your light, and your power to such an extent that events that used to make you feel little or helpless or out of control, no longer touch you as they may have in the past. (One day, they will not affect you at all). And it means you must, you *must*, be aware of and acknowledge your growth.

 ## Discuss and/or Journal

1. List the characteristics of a warrior, as *you* believe them to be. (Don't be too unrealistic.)
2. Now jot down how each characteristic applies to you on this journey. Can you see yourself—no, *feeeeel* yourself—as that warrior you described? If not right now, can you feel it coming?
3. Describe how it feels to be a champion of the Light. Can you see yourself in that role? Let us hope so, for indeed, good friend, that is exactly what you are!

Principle #2 Until we ask, nothing happens

Just like firing up a Want, until we learn that it's okay to *ask*, nothing is going to happen. It's a habit we need to get into and never, ever let go. In this segment we're going to focus on more esoteric things that have to do with spiritual enrichment. And please, that is *not* to say that Wants are not spiritual, for after all, what isn't spiritual? We are simply going to focus here on obtaining that wonderful feeling of being spiritually connected or plugged in—and knowing it—through asking, the most crucial step to our empowerment.

Indeed, until we ask, nothing can happen, for this is a free-will universe. Not one cosmic "hand" can be lifted until we ask, but when we ask (not plead or beg or implore) in the high energy of appreciation, all the powers of the universe unite to answer our call, providing we allow it. *But we must ask!*

If we ask to be filled with a presence that allows us to appreciate everything we see and every thought we think, it happens. If we ask for guidance, we will receive it. If we ask to feel the love of our Entity, we will feel it. If we ask for ways to increase our income, we will receive those ways. If we ask to have joy in our life, we will have it. If our Desire is to know our True Selves, we become a dynamo of power simply through the asking, because the high frequencies of our Godhood are released within us to form a new knowing, a new sense of Self. In just the simple act of asking in reverence, we raise our frequencies.

And so, ask to be filled with those things your soul longs for. Every morning before you begin your day, find a time to ask. And then keep on asking—for love, compassion, peace, and joy. Put your awareness in your heart center, and *feeeeel* those things. Ask to be filled with a consciousness that will allow you to love everything you see and every thought you think, and it will begin to happen. Ask to expand, and you will start to pull a higher energy vortex into your body, creating an actual cellular, physical energy change. Ask to give up all remaining negativity, all old and unnecessary beliefs, all limited thinking. When respect and reverence are present in our requests, all heaven stands ready to rush in with answers and assistance. Ask occasionally, and you will be heard. Ask *daily* and you will be answered, for you fill the heavens with your light.

> When you are sensitive to the way you feel, you always have the benefit of Guidance.

"Me calling universe . . . me to universe . . . do you read?"

Inside each God-self-directed antenna, write out one of your deepest spiritual Desires. This may take some thought, so don't be discouraged if nothing comes to mind at first. (Note examples on the opposite page.) When you are finished, transfer these desires to your "Weekly Spiritual Ask List" on the next page.

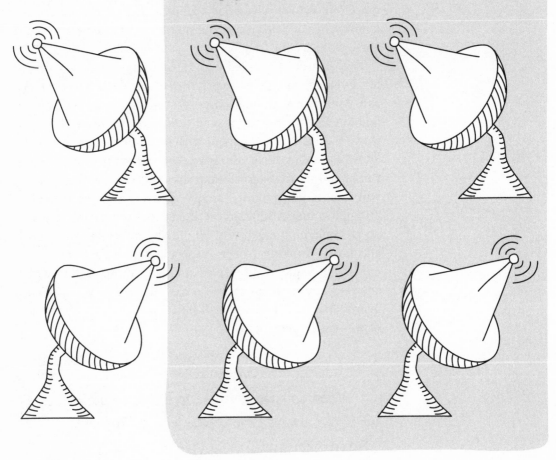

My Weekly Spiritual Ask List

*Knowing ahead of time what's on your morning Ask List is a huge help. In this exercise, make a short, weekly list of only three or four things of a spiritual nature to ask for in your morning meditation, including all of the items from the previous page, and more if you think of them. Just as in projecting your Wants, feeeeel what you are asking for. Gear your lists to your spiritual growth. Then, taking time in the morning to explain **each one out loud** will help you into the desired feeling.*

In the asking is the presumption of receipt.

Week One
(e.g., I ask for signs that I am guided)

Week Two
(e.g., I ask for awakening)

Week Three
(e.g., I ask that I recognize my lessons)

Week Four
(e.g., teach me how to feel my own love)

Week Five

Week Six

Principle #3 Passion is creation

How passionate are you about your Desires, be they spiritual, material, or physical? How deeply committed are you to receiving what you asked for? Remember, you are far more than your body: You are the eternal power of the universe. Passion accesses that power. Even that which you believe is not possible becomes possible when your energy flow matches your Desire, which is why passion is creation.

But it takes being a warrior to become passionate about something you think impossible. If your Desire is going in one direction, and your energy is going in another direction, passion goes out the window along with your connection to your Source energy. Then comes frustration and/or depression or withdrawal from the pure positive energy of your Expanded Self.

So how passionate are you? Where would you put yourself on this scale regarding your askings, your Wants, your Desires? How much resistance do you have to your own high, pure energy?

Valve pretty well closed to God-self energy
↓

| **Anger** Strong desire *and* strong resistance | **Frustration** Desire is present, but so is resistance | **Peace** Contentment, *not much Desire*, but still no resistance | **Passion** Excitement, *strong Desire*, enthusiasm, and *no resistance* |

Valve wide open to God-self energy ↗

Passion is nothing more than divinely pumped-up emotion. It is blatant, unrestricted happiness going after a Want with intense magnetism. So how do you get it? How do you get your juices running over wanting to become something for which social consciousness ridicules you, or when the so-called odds are against you?

The answer is to *make* yourself plug into your joy, your excitement, your knowing, your Inner Being, your Expanded Self, your God-self, and *demand* that you stay there long enough to create more passion. Then give more time to your Desires, and more time, and more time. The more time you give to them, the more passion will flow, and the bigger and stronger those vortexes will become. The bigger the vortexes become, the more passion you will feel. And the more passionate you feel, the faster your Desires will manifest. Heaven on earth begins with passion. If you can't work up a sweat over your Desire, start small. Think about it over and over until thinking about it makes you feel good. Pretty soon, you've built a bridge between your Desire and your old beliefs that say, "This is bunk." As your passion builds, so does your connection with your God-self. Powerful, passionate Desire and excitement—that is being plugged into your God-consciousness!

> Passion is
> God-self in
> action.

My Passion Thermometer

If we don't know where we are, we'll never know where we're going. This exercise will take guts, because it calls for brutal honesty. Find twelve of your Wants from any chapter, including your Weekly Spiritual Ask List, and search your soul to honestly position them on your Passion Thermometer, meaning how passionate you are about them and how much time you give them with an open valve. Do not berate yourself if they don't all fall into the top spot. This is only for evaluation, not for self-condemnation. There are no mistakes, only new awareness.

I'm passionate about:

continued . . .

I'm so-so with:

I'm frustrated over:

I'm angry about:

 Discuss and/or Journal

It takes a spiritual
warrior to be
passionate about
the impossible.

1. Take a look at the kind of Wants that were placed in each spot. See if you can find a pattern of the type of Wants you're most passionate about, all the way down to those you're flat-out angry about.

2. How many of your meaningful Wants did you neglect to mention at all? Why do you suppose that is? You might say, "Not enough room on the page." Really? Could you have made room? Are your Wants just too big or too impossible for you to believe they could happen?

3. If that's so—that you didn't list some Wants because they are too "impossible"—please now make a list of all the reasons why you think those Wants could never happen.

Please note: There is absolutely nothing wrong with being so-so about anything or frustrated or even angry. Anger and frustration can be grand motivators. But if you stay in that energy, flowing out those low vibrations about your Wants, all you're doing is making sure you never get them—not to mention how you're negatively affecting every other area of your life!

4. Looking over that list, what does that say about your belief in the power of You, or about your belief in the creative force you actually are? Better take a long, hard look at this one, then decide how you are going to overcome those very negative, limiting thoughts. For instance, do your Wants all have to come right now? Can you believe—even a little—that one day they may be possible? Do you trust your Guidance?

5. Why did you place any Wants at all in the "so-so" box? If you want these things, be they spiritual, physical, emotional, material, or all four, why do you think you are so-so or at peace or flatlining about them? Would it be better for you to remove them altogether? Or could you get passionate about them? If not, what are you resisting?

6. What's the difference between your frustration and your anger? How do they differ in feeling? In intensity?

7. How do you see passion as being creation? What does that really mean to you? Can you *feeeeel* what that means?

8. How would you start small with your biggest Want? How could you begin to trust that your own power could, indeed, make this happen?

Principle #4   We always, *always* have choices

How often do you feel trapped or boxed in? You feel like there's no way out, nowhere to turn, often no one to turn *to*. That's when we need to stretch our God-consciousness, and *choose* our way out of the box.

The reason we feel trapped is that we cannot see we have choices. If we feel we have no choice, we are living as a victim under the control of social-consciousness energy, that low-frequency, negative stuff that says, "This is the way it's always been and will always be."

You know that you are more than your body. You know, now, that you create from vibrational frequency. You know that nothing affects your experience other than the way you are flowing your energy. So here is what we need to remember—*must remember*—if we intend to stretch our God-consciousness daily:

1. We always have choices.
2. If we can't find answers, it means we have overlooked the obvious.
3. We have options. What are they? *"What are my options?"*
4. To find them, we must plug in to our Guidance, and ask.
5. Once we find them, all we have to do is flow energy to them.

If you are in a situation you don't like and don't know what to do, if ever there was a time to expand your God-consciousness, this is it! When you're in such a situation, whether of long standing or not, look at it like so:

1. This is the result or my own energy flow.
2. I do not have to like it or approve of it.
3. I do not want to add to it by focusing negatively on it.
4. I know I have choices, that there are alternatives.
5. "From the light or God that I an, I call out for those choices to be revealed to me."
6. Now I will listen, and I will write.
7. I won't try to pound it into place.
8. I won't fly into Hi Ho Silvering action.
9. Instead, I will find my many choices, and ...
   — flow my energy to the one I presently Desire.
   — begin Inspired Action in vibrational harmony with Who and What I really am.
10. If the alternative I chose is not satisfactory, I will call for more.

In times of trial, *feeeeel* to yourself "I choose love."

We are free beings, but until we realize that we have options in life, we will never be able to experience that freedom. So whenever a feeling of being trapped comes over you, call an immediate halt to everything, go inside, ask for guidance, and begin to listen for the choices that are always, always available.

My "Which Way to Go" Exercise: Part I

Choices and decisions go hand in hand: first comes the choice, then comes the decision to "go" or "no go." How do we know if the choice we've made is the best one for us? Can we be sure? Yes, but only by feeling.

The easy way to do this exercise is simply to take a major decision that's facing you now, make a sizable list of your options, then see how each one feels by mentally placing it first into the "Yes" column, then into the "No" column, checking out how each one (Yes or No) feels as you go along.

The wrinkle to be aware of here is when we come up with the only possible choice and it still feels lousy. For example, maybe you have elderly parents who now need care. You've listed all your options but find that none of them feel good. What do you do then? You go for the one that feels the best, even if it doesn't feel terrific. There's a difference between a "No" that shouts to you, and a "Yes, this is right," even if that "Yes" doesn't sing. In this case, perhaps it means having to find a nursing home. If that feels better than having your parents live with you, then that's your answer.

List three major problems or challenges facing you now, describing your worries or concerns regarding them. Then, on the next page, pick only one of those decisions or problems you are facing now and write out your choices. You've probably already thought of some choices, so before you begin, ask your Guidance for assistance in finding more, lots more. There are always more!

One decision I'm facing is:

continued . . .

Another decision I'm facing is:

Another decision I'm facing is:

My "Which Way to Go" Exercise: Part II

Our goal, of course, is to find the yes choice that feels the best. There will always be a no choice that feels the worst.

Taking one decision from the previous page, list all the options you can think of first. Then, beginning at the top of the list, slowly go inside to feeeeel each one. Feel it with a YES, then with a NO. Let your answers to this one be colorful, e.g., "terrific," "awful," etc. Take your time, and feeeel!

The decision I'm facing is:		
List all options first:	If I say YES to this one, how does it feel?	If I say NO to this one, how does it feel?
Throw my parents off the bridge	Kinda nice	Better

continued . . .

List all options first:	If I say YES to this one, how does it feel?	If I say NO to this one, how does it feel?

Yeah but...what if I make the wrong choice?

Number one: You can't. Number two: So what? Number three: You chose that one to learn from, so what's the lesson? Number four: You'll probably live to choose again! If not, that's how you and your Entity planned it. So go for it!

Since we're talking about choice, we had better talk about **what-ifs**. There are two kinds of what-ifs, and both apply to choice. A negative what-if is pure worry: "What if I fail?" "What if I run out of money?" Whereas a positive what-if is high-frequency energy flow engaged when making the choices: "What if I did it this way?" "What if I went there?"

My choice is:

Closed Valve:

I blow it?

fear

concern

worry

—————— What if? ——————

Open Valve:

I could find an investor?

excitement

enthusiasm

thrill

The *Don't You Dare Skip This One* Exercise

The ability to make choices with ease comes as a result of how many neuro-pathways have been created in the brain. The fastest way to create new neuro-pathways is to *force* choices. Normally, when faced with a decision, we stop after only ten or twelve options, thinking there are no more.

With this very difficult exercise, you will find you've probably run out of options around the fourteen or fifteen mark. That is when you must push. This may take several days, even weeks, but you'll know when you've hit the breakthrough, for ideas will begin to flow again. Keep going! *With each new idea you push out, you are creating a fantastic new network in your brain.*

Write your most sincere Want. Now, you must list eighty-eight ways to accomplish that. Go for kooky, far-out, nuts, crazy, and list them all. It will seem utterly impossible, but you can do it! *Call on your Guidance, relax, and allow. This is one of the most important exercises in this book for pushing us into the awareness of our divine capabilities. (It was as a result of doing this exercise that I altered the format of my mortgage company into a virtual moneymaking machine.)*

Note! You MAY NOT use any ideas you've already had!

My want is:		
1.		
2.		
3.		
4.		
5.		

continued . . .

6.

7.

8.

9.

10.

11.

12.

13.

14.

15.

16.

17.

18.

19.

20.

Don't stop now!

21.

22.

23.

24.

continued . . .

25.

26.

27.

28.

29.

30.

Push yourself!

31.

32.

33.

34.

35.

36.

37.

38.

39.

40.

41.

42.

43.

continued . . .

44.

45.

46.

47.

48.

49.

50.

51.

52.

53.

54.

55.

56.

57.

58.

59.

60.

61.

62.

No matter how crazy WRITE IT DOWN!

continued . . .

63.

64.

65.

66.

67.

68.

69.

70.

71.

72.

73.

74.

75.

76.

77.

78.

79.

80.

81.

Reach, reach, REACH!!!

Let your imagination go WILD!

continued . . .

82. _____

83. _____

84. _____

85. _____

86. _____

87. _____

88. _____

Come on, you're almost done...just a few more!

More on Choices

The universe is abundant, so are our choices

The universe doesn't understand our limitations, pain, or anguish. Problems? Yes. Challenges? Sure, the universe has challenges galore, so it goes to work on its choices. Let's be like the universe and *know* that we have free will and an abundance of choices. When we feel we have no choice, we are simply avoiding the responsibility of—and therefore the *joy* of—life. Be free! Look for choices.

Choices can be about our feelings as well as about events. We choose what we think about. Often anger can be just plain fun, so we consciously choose that. But if a negative emotion is not conscious, it is not a choice, and we're in for trouble. *We* are the only ones who choose our day-to-day emotions, no one else—not our mate, not our boss, not our kids, not our friends, not the rain. As we remember that we make ourselves, moment by moment, out of our emotional responses, it would behoove us to pay attention to our choice of feelings!

Learn to think in the language of abundance

By our own choice we return again and again to negative events, and they grow larger. How much control is an event having in your life right now? Then ask yourself how much energy you are giving to it. Don't like what's happening? Find new choices, then change the energy. *Change the energy!!!* The way out of anything is *know* you have choices. Then don't dillydally. Choose one! Be free! Find your hidden choices.

If we don't like what we have, we have only to remove our focus from it, find new choices, flow our energy to our pick, then expect it to happen. It's that simple!

> God-consciousness offers choices; touching that means freedom.

Principle #5 The best use of our time is learning to flow our energy constructively

The daily practice of "turning on," meaning flowing out our open valve energy to stretch our God-consciousness, is what will turn the daily-living tide for us. But for "turning on" to have any effect, we need to do it often—at work, in the car, in the subway, brushing our teeth, mowing the lawn.

The more we stretch to those higher universal frequencies, the more we'll change electromagnetically. The more we change electromagnetically, the happier we'll be. The happier we become, the faster our manifestations will come. The faster our manifestations come, the happier we'll be.

Remember, if it's negative emotion, it's strictly third-dimensional and physical. If it's positive feelings, it's the pure positive energy of our God-self, the same stuff that runs the universe. That's what we're after. That's what we want running our bodies and our lives, and that's what we must consciously stretch to obtain, every moment of every day that we can possibly remember to do it.

But just like revitalizing an unused muscle, our consciousness will only get where we want it to be by stretching it—a

little today, a little more tomorrow, a little more the next day—
until stretching becomes a habit,

until we can know in an instant, by how we feel, what kind of energy we're flowing out, therefore, what we're attracting,

until we can Flip-Switch from negative to positive flow in a heartbeat,

until we can watch the world around us crumble, and know that all is well,

until we can flow appreciation and love and wonder to *anyone, anytime,*

until we can *allow* our Desires to manifest,

until we can laugh at the lessons of contrast,

until we understand, without the tiniest shadow of doubt, that we have created it all, from the most ghastly to the most fantastic,

until we can know, from the depths of our beings, that we are never alone,

until we know that no one, dead or alive, is now or ever has been any greater than our very own Self,

until we can manifest our Desires in shorter and shorter increments of time,

until we can look at death and feel the joy of rebirth into one's God-self,

until we can stand with the strength and knowing of a true master,

until all of our old, destructive beliefs no longer deter our well-being, until we live more often than not from our divine intuition,

until we know the universe and ourselves are one.

Until we arrive at these places—which we can do very soon—we stretch and stretch and stretch our God-consciousness, daily. And even then, we stretch!

We live as we vibrate, not as we decide.

HOMEWORK! *(Learning to do What?)*
Play…play…PLAY!!!

Hang on to your hats!!! Did you know that playing raises your frequencies and stretches God-consciousness? When you play, you're in joy, pushing your frequencies way up off the charts.

Are you aware of how little you play? Do you think you could find ways to do it more? We're talking serious play here, not just things that bring you joy, like gardening. Things like playing ball, sailing, playing marbles, going to a game, hiking with friends. If bridge or chess is really play for you, well, okay. But what we're looking for here is free-floating, balls-to-the-wall, let-it-all-hang-out play. For a quick test, list your six most favorite things to play at, and then jot down when you last did them. Lesson? Learn to play more!

Some things I love to play at are:	The last time I did this was:

MORE HOMEWORK! *LOOK UP* ↑

Sound crazy? No way! The actual act of taking your eyes from the ground and casting them to the skies (or even the ceiling) will raise your frequencies. Looking down freezes you into physicality and social consciousness. Looking up sends your mind—and therefore your frequencies—to search for the bigger picture. So change your gaze from low to high. It's a real God-consciousness stretcher.

EVEN MORE HOMEWORK!
Ongoing, Forevermore

If you're gotten this far, you're completely committed to creating your own Heaven on Earth and to living as the God you are while in a body. To accomplish that, stretching God-consciousness daily is the number one requirement.

Here's a short recap of only a few of the things that will open your valve, raise your frequencies, and stretch your God-consciousness. Please! Practice at least one or more of these daily, along with anything else that will pull in the strong positive energy of the exquisite Entity you are.

A few of the things that stretch my God-consciousness are:	I do this DAILY	I do this SOME-TIMES	I do this RARELY	I NEVER do this
Searching for ways to feel good				
Laughing				
Asking...for whatever				
Jump starting with my inner smile				

continued . . .

A few of the things that stretch my God-consciousness are:	I do this DAILY	I do this SOME-TIMES	I do this RARELY	I NEVER do this
Doing these five things from my Joy List				
1.				
2.				
3.				
4.				
5.				
Flip-Switching				
Scripting...about any-thing				
Feeling my wants				
Turning on just to turn on				
Flowing appreciation to anything				
Marveling at the little things				
Listening for my Guid-ance and trusting it				
Flowing energy before acting				

Waves of Transformation

Listen to yourself take several slow, deep breaths. Once again, pull up emerald-green light from the center of Mother Earth . . . wrap it around you . . . then send it from your heart out around the planet and back to enfold you in its healing energy.

You're walking on a sunny beach. The air is sweet with the smell of saltwater and fresh breezes. Under your feet is the whitest, cleanest sand you've ever seen. Above, small puffy clouds dance against a deep blue backdrop. The day is spectacular, the moment beautiful. You are filled with timeless joy.

And now, lay your body down on the warm, soft sand, close enough to the water so that the waves will wash over your entire body. The water is very warm as it spills over you, and you feel caressed, nurtured, loved. You lie there completely relaxed, fully trusting, and in profound joy.

The ocean has now turned into liquid Light, so that as the next wave rolls over you, it engulfs you with its brilliant effervescence. Feel the Light . . . feel the love . . . feel the universe washing over you, pouring Light through every cell of your body. As the wave of Light ebbs, it is pulling out all resistance to change and growth, all resistance to transformation, all resistance to empowerment.

Another wave of Light comes to wash over you and through you. Feel yourself surrender

> **INSIGHT**
> True Life is letting go of limitations.

to its love, to its power, to its joy. As it pulls away, feel all desire to hold on to past negativities leave with it, washing those low energies forever back into the bottomless sea of liquid love.

Another wave of liquid Light comes, washing over and through you. Feel it. Allow it. The wave pulls away. What did it give you? What did it take back with it into the sea of divine forgiveness that is You?

Tenet Twelve

We approve of ourselves, no matter what

**WITH THIS TENET
WE LEARN**

o that finding out how to love Self is why
  we came here

o that learning how to approve of
  ourselves is where we begin

o to overcome all areas of self-hate,
  doubt, and approval-seeking

o how to find the true, pure love we have
  sought for so very long

Principle #1 Negative self-judgment kills the body

We've heard it until we want to throw up: "Now now, you must learn to approve of yourself." "Yeah? Who says, and what for? If it makes me feel good to beat up on myself, why shouldn't I?"

Well, there are two basic reasons why it's time to quit that game:

1. Negative self-judgment causes illness.
2. Negative self-judgment keeps us from what we came here to learn.

Illness

This one is big! Every time we judge anything about ourselves, the body goes on instant alert, having just been told that something is wrong with it. The moment that alarm is sounded, the ever-faithful body goes instantly into its DNA genetic *and* "soulular" (meaning all the "yous" that have ever existed) data bank, back countless generations, to find anything it can that might be a match from the past to whatever it's just been told is wrong with it now. Then it brings that "wrong" forward for healing. "Here you are, Master, I just found something you now call 'cancer' from a thousand lifetimes ago. Since you felt the same about that as you do about what is wrong now, I see those feelings match, so I'm bringing it up for you to heal. Oh good, Master, perhaps we'll be all right now."

Not likely! Now you've got the potential for cancer in the body just because you made a negative judgment about your weight, while your loving body thinks it's doing you a favor. Every time you negatively judge *anything* about yourself, from attitude to physical appearance, the body will rush in to help by providing a matching vibration from your genetic past for you to now heal. If you hated cancer a thousand lifetimes ago as much as you now hate your weight, yippee, the body found a match to pull up so you can heal it. That means every time you tell the body it's wrong, you create the potential for illness.

Facing our own Love

Empowerment, enlightenment, and awakening will elude us forever until we can stand in the presence of our own Love—our own Entity, Inner Being, Expanded Self—without running. Until we allow ourselves to touch that Love, feel that Love, be that Love, our journey in physicality will never be complete.

Self-denigration is not only a deadly game, it says we do not believe our divinity, our beauty, our vitality, our creativity, our perfection, our joyousness, the very essences of the Gods we are. Rather, self-judgment tells us we are "second rate" and "less than."

Self-condemnation in *any* form is nothing but a cop-out, a comfortable place to be where we have no responsibility to our True Selves, only to our physical images. We can meditate, chant, play with crystals and incense, do yoga exercises, and proclaim our divinity forevermore, but for as long as we hold judgments against ourselves, empowerment and awakening will be nothing but words.

Why do we find it so hard to approve of ourselves? Why do we continue to reproach, criticize, nitpick, punish, condemn, shame, and belittle ourselves? Because if we did not, we would be left with having to touch our own Love. And the touching of that Love would mean the melting of our images. And we still think that the melting of our images would mean the loss of our security.

There is within each of us a power and awareness that, when found and felt, creates a knowing, a calm, a sureness, and a place of safety where we no longer have the need to hide behind our comfortable insecurities. Our job is to find that place and expand it into true empowerment.

Self-criticism is a killer because it locks us inside our bodies. It closes our valve, washing us in the most caustic, destructive negative energies that can be produced. Lack of self-love is another expression for judgment, creating negative energy that closes in upon itself.

No Wants or manifestations can come to you while you are—in any way—disapproving of yourself. No abundance, no well-being, no perfect health, and very little joy. To the degree that you hold yourself in low esteem you will know unhappiness and misery, for not only is self-judgment a valve closer, it is the most potently toxic energy that has ever been created—anywhere.

Let It All Hang Out Exercise

Regarding our Don't Wants, our first step is to recognize that we have them—in abundance! Yes, you surely have done an exercise like this before, but this time you're tapping into Guidance.

Fill *the energy ring that surrounds you (below) with your known negative self-judgments. Then go inside to your Inner Being, ask to be taken deeper, listen, and write those areas of self-condemnation you prefer to ignore or deny: physical attributes, thoughts, actions/reactions, big or small. Anything and everything!*

What I don't like about me is:

my nose

my fear of speaking up

And Now, the I Approve of Them Exercise

Okay, so you've got a big batch of Don't Wants and Don't Likes about yourself. Good for you for spotting them. Now see what it feels like to *approve* of them!

List some of the most potent items from the previous page, and find the feeling of the thing you listed (like... yuck!). Then wrap the item in appreciation for the lesson it has given you. No matter how bad, how awful, how rank, how old, how tiresome this thing is, **find the approval of it.** *Make yourself stay with the approval of that item until you can feel the release from "yuck" to "it's okay!" The high frequency of approval disperses the low frequency of disapproval, opening your valve to you. So put forth the most powerful intent you can muster to approve of yourself and all that you have done, been, or felt,* **no matter what.** *The universe approves of you unconditionally; who are you to disagree?!*

> Find the approval. Find the approval. Find the approval.

Make your list first, then go to your feelings.

The thing I listed	How thinking about it makes feel	How approving of it makes me feel

Principle #2   Nothing outside of Self can bring peace

We do it all day long, don't we? Not only is it part of our heritage, it is ingrained within all of humanity. And what is "it"? Seeking approval outside of ourselves—a sad result of our not knowing Who and What we truly are.

If we are to walk into our empowerment where freedom of existence reigns supreme, where we live with compassion for all mankind without being chained by "shoulds," where we know that love of Self is the force of the universe—the thing of which worlds are made—then we must find a way to stop seeking approval outside of ourselves. Now, frankly, I doubt we'll ever stop this insidious practice completely, but we *can* rid ourselves of at least 75 percent of our former approval seeking, for, up to now, much of it has been unconscious.

> When a human couches their creation in the arena of approval or allowance outside of Self, so it is this human addresses Self as limited.

We can no longer seek outside what we must learn to give to ourselves from the inside, for validation-seeking is closed valve stuff. The moment we begin to fish around for approval outside of ourselves, we're swimming in negative energy, flowing out highly magnetic streams of lack-oriented vibrations.

When we can look at ourselves in the mirror in full approval and say, "You are who you are, kid, and I'm learning to love every funny little thing about you just the way you are," we're on our way! When we no longer have to bathe ourselves in perfume, or tiptoe on eggs before speaking, or dress for the identity of lusty macho, femme fatale, or true cool, we're on our way. When we can look in that mirror and say from the depths of our being, "Hell no, I'd never want to do that again, but I no longer have any regrets about it," not only are we are on our way to empowerment, we no longer have to react from guilt or shame in order to please the whole world.

Finding the Love that we are is mandatory. That's it! End of lesson! Learning to feel it, know it, be it, and act—not REact—from that vibration must be our only focused goal.

> We must find ways to approve of ourselves first, instead of looking outside of us.

Everything else we have done to raise our frequencies and open our valves has only been practice toward this end. Now we're down to it. This is what our entire lives have been about: learning to love and cherish the beauty, the preciousness, the magnificence, the spectacular divinity that we are.

No one is suggesting we run around nude, or make love in the middle of Times Square. There are certain social graces to which we prefer adhering. All we're doing now is finding ways to walk out of our fear of rejection, for in the final analysis, that is the primary reason we do not approve of ourselves. And every fear, no matter how big or small, closes our valve and cuts us off from our God-self.

 ## Discuss and/or Journal

1. Until we approve of ourselves, we seek the approval of others.
2. We think we are not worthy, because...
3. We think we do not measure up, because...
4. We are afraid to speak up, because...
5. We still regret what we did, because...
6. We still feel guilty, because...
7. We try to please "them," because...
8. "Because" is an excuse that causes us to vibrate—and feel—how?
9. Why do we continue to berate ourselves?
10. Talk (write) about how it *feeeeels* when you are approval-seeking or reaching for validation.
11. What is the difference between acting from defiance and from a place of self-approval? How do those differences feel?

The "Dump It" Exercise

Fill up the page with approval-seeking things you do that you're ready to toss in the trash. They can be things you say to put yourself down, things you dislike about the way you act or think, ways you dress or speak, people-pleasing things you do. Find all you can, but do not get down on yourself about what you find. We're getting it turned around.

> Until we can trust the miracle of what we are, we will always be looking to others for approval.

I agree with people when I don't want to.

Principle #3 Judge the road you've traveled, and you judge the God you are

o First comes judgment of ourselves in the way we act, look, and think.

o Then, since we don't like the way we act, look, or think, we reach outside of ourselves for others to approve of us, since we can't (or won't).

o Then we judge all those awful things we've done in our past.

o Then we judge our judgments.

> When we can live without regrets, the worst of our negative energy will be gone.

If we are to become deliberate creators, flowing whatever we may call "the good life" all about us, then we must learn to approve of everything we've ever done. *Everything!* We've got to stop seeing every little thing we did as a mistake or blunder, or even as an embarrassment. We must—we absolutely must—learn to release the guilt. How? By remembering that everything we ever did, we did for the experience of it.

Mistake? No such thing! Failure? No such thing! Yes, you may have been a horse's ass. So what?! Cut yourself some slack. Get off your case. Flip-Switch out of that focus, or you're sure to repeat the act or something similar.

Regrets, guilt, remorse; call it what you will, that energy is the most destructive, useless, stagnant energy of the universe. That kind of energy brings a halt to everything, including your life! It is the denial of the God-self within you. Living with regrets or guilt is living life with a totally closed valve.

True self-acceptance is saying to yourself—*in spite of* all the awful things you've done, *in spite of* all the things you feel guilty for, *in spite of* all your faults and imperfections, *in spite of* all your little secrets and fearful uglies you're terrified to admit to yourself—"It's all right, it's all right, *it's all right.*"

Ask for help from those who walk with you. Tender-talk yourself, tough-talk yourself, write new scripts about how you *want* to feel. Assure yourself that everything is a cocreation to get beyond the "I did it to them" syndrome. Write about it in a form of approval until you can think or talk about it without the sting. Then you have owned it. If you can't think about it without the sting, then flood it with love until you can. Empowerment can only manifest in the present, never—but *never*—from the past! So emblazon this into your head: No regrets. No regrets. *I have NO regrets!*

> No regrets, no regrets, no regrets. Get off your case, like now. Don't forgive it; forget it! Let 'em go. Give 'em up. Then let your feelings be your guide.

YES, I DID IT!

The "I'm Done with It" Exercise

Pick just one thing from your past you still regret. Then, beginning at the top, write a statement that makes you feel a little better about it (only a little better!). Then find a statement that can make you feeeeel even better about it, and write it out in the next box. Keep going, box by box, finding statements where you can feeeeel better and better about what you did, until you get to the bottom box. Now find a statement where there is no sting, no gripping in your gut, only a feeeeeling of complete freedom. **"YES! I did it, I own it, and now I can let it go!"**

Principle #4 Learning to give to Self breaks down lifetimes of barriers

"Better to give than to receive?" Not on a bet! "But isn't it selfish to put yourself first, before all others?" No, it is not. In fact, until we can learn *how* to give to ourselves and feel worthy enough to receive, giving to others is just an act of people-pleasing coming from a closed valve desire for approval.

The principle of Giving to Self is extraordinarily difficult—at first. "Don't take," "don't want," "squash your desires," "stop being selfish," "what you get can only equal what you give;" these are all statements designed centuries ago by powerful organizations that wanted to control. And they have worked brilliantly. We feel shame and guilt when we give to ourselves. We feel sinful to want, and unworthy to have, all of which serves only to heighten our lack of respect for ourselves.

There is no greater job we have while on this planet than to walk into a full and noble respect of our divine Selves. There is no greater purpose in this life than to find ways to live for the love and fulfillment of Self. And these can only be achieved by making the decision to cut loose, once and for all, our habitual, yet totally unnecessary feelings of unworthiness.

Every insecurity or feeling of unworthiness you have, every perceived limitation, every hurt ever incurred, every sorrow, everything that irritates you about you, embrace them all and love them like you've never loved anything in your entire life, because when you love your own self-judgments, you own them into wisdom. You go from a perpetually closed valve, straight into joy.

Yes, we've talked about giving to ourselves by learning how to turn on our desires and intents. But we haven't as yet related the *lack* of self-giving to our unending need for approval. When we *repeatedly* say that giving to others gives us more joy than giving to ourselves, we'd better take another look, for that is nothing more than fear hiding behind a frightened, self-righteous mask. Open valve happiness is the ability to be free of insecurities and the need to please. And it comes, first and foremost, by allowing the realization that we are, indeed, worthy to receive whatever in this universe will give us joy, no matter how small, no matter how large, no matter how outrageous or meaningless to others.

Your every emotion creates your life. Get rid of those that cause you pain.

> Your God-self gives you that which you believe you are worth, and nothing more.

One more thing on giving to Self: learn to allow!

To approve of ourselves, the order of the day is to lighten up, chill out, get mellow, calm down, relax, go natural, stop worrying, cool it, slow down, take it easy, be gentle with ourselves, and...

allow, allow, *ALLOW!*

o Allow (and honor) your negative emotions, then change them.

o Allow (and honor) your down moods, then change them when you're ready.

o Allow (and honor) your goofs; they are what you came here to learn from.

o Allow (and honor) your old unworthiness, then love it out of your life.

o Allow your body to be what it is, then, if you want to change it, start scripting.

o Allow you to be wherever you are in life; you created it for a reason.

o Allow (and honor) your past, no matter what it is; you manifested it for the emotional wisdom.

> Allow yourself to know that what you are within yourself is valuable enough to let go of what inhibits purposeful happiness and joy within your life.

HOMEWORK

The likelihood of you actually doing this exercise is probably between zip and nil. After all, it does require a sizable investment of time and effort to purchase the poster board, draw your lines, get the stars, and remember to paste them up. For months! Not to mention that you'll surely have some not-too-pleasant reactions to feeling like you're back in grade school.

Nonetheless, if you have any hang-ups about giving yourself joys, if it's easy for you to buy a $100 gift for someone else but you can't spend $17.95 on yourself, if other people always come first, you need to take a long, hard look at how little respect you have for yourself. Without self-respect, you can toss this whole program out the window, because you're turning your back on your own divinity. Self-respect is the cornerstone of empowerment!

The first step in acquiring self-respect is to push out pain, loneliness, and struggle. And the fastest way to do that is to leap over society's hurdle that says, "There is nothing spiritual about being rich or having fun or thoroughly enjoying one's self." Ridiculous! Your very *job*, as a divine piece of All That Is, is learning to do and be what pleases your heart, soul, and body. The more you give to yourself in joy, the more you become the You of you. For joy is what God is!

As childish as I thought this exercise was, the results were phenomenal. Working almost daily with this simple grade-school poster up on my wall was the only thing—the *only* thing—that finally broke me out of the fear of my own joy. It taught me how to say "No" to "them," "yes" to me, and how at long last to feel the exquisite thrill of giving to myself. I cannot urge you strongly enough to do this. IT will put you in touch with your God-self faster than anything else you could possibly do. Okay, here's how it works.

Buy a box of stars and a 24" x 28" piece of poster board, drawing it up to match the following table. Use whatever headings you want; these are just suggestions.

The first day you put up a star, you feel elation. Then you find out how long it takes to put up another one, and how often you deny yourself various pleasures. You see patterns unfolding, like blanks under things you like to do or nothing happening on Mondays.

Soon you're looking for ways to give to yourself so you can put more stars up on your silly board. When that happens, brace yourself, for you've absolutely broken those self-denying patterns, and your stuck floodgates are beginning to open for you to receive the abundance you have been flowing out so faithfully and vigorously. Watch you patterns, make yourself break out of them, and in just a few months you'll be walking into a new life.

	Mon	Tue	Wed	Thu	Fri	Sat	Sun

Physical

	Mon	Tue	Wed	Thu	Fri	Sat	Sun
Did something from Joy List							
Dining out, movies, or ?							
Any other kind of play							
Body care							
Had friends over							
Bought something for me							

Emotional

	Mon	Tue	Wed	Thu	Fri	Sat	Sun
Tough-talked to self							
Tender-talked to self							
Flooded myself with gratitude							

	Mon	Tue	Wed	Thu	Fri	Sat	Sun
Allowed some ugly feelings							
Flip-Switched							
Marveled at anything							

Mental

	Mon	Tue	Wed	Thu	Fri	Sat	Sun
Called for guidance							
Felt my thoughts							
Decided I have a choice							
Intended on something							
Listed more Wants							
Noticed more Don't Wants							

Spiritual

	Mon	Tue	Wed	Thu	Fri	Sat	Sun
Felt my Guidance							
Sat and felt my Love							
Listened to my inner knowing							
Asked for Love							
Saw God in another							
Became part of nature							

Principle #5   Loving of Self and approving of Self are one and the same

"We *must* learn to love ourselves." Doesn't that phrase just make you want to throw up? "Yes, you nitwits, I'd be happy to love myself if someone would just show me how!"

And yet love of one's Self is indeed mandatory if we are to become empowered, if we are to live a Heaven on Earth while in this body, if we are to find greater happiness, freedom, and well-being. Why? Because loving ourselves, *which is nothing more than approving of ourselves*, makes us feel good. The better we feel, the higher our vibrations. The higher our vibrations, the faster we manifest, the more we allow in to our world, and the happier we will be. The happier we are … etc., etc.

The bottom line is this: The greater the love grows with us, the greater and faster our abundance and well-being will manifest. And the more it manifests, the more unlimited we become, meaning empowered, closer to our divinity, in touch with our God-selves, and frankly, in love with life.

Take our bodies, for instance. We created them just the way we wanted them to be in order to learn from them whatever is up for us to learn, yet all we do is gripe about them. Instead, if we would come to terms with our bodies and say, "All right, maybe I can't play tight end for the Packers or win the Miss Universe contest; maybe I can't do some things I'd like to, but what I opted for when I came in here is perfect in its own state of being." When we can say that, we've leapfrogged to a new level of approval of our God-self, not just our physical self.

Our bodies were created out of pure, incomprehensible love, a love we can touch, feel, and become. But first we have to find that pure love within us. It's not a place; it's a feeling, a feeling tone. It's the beauty we are, the preciousness, the sweetness, the love, the power, the eternal joy, and yes, even the impishness. Ask to go there, so that your body and your God-self can begin merging into one.

Why were you drawn to this book? Why are you so into knowing all this off-the-wall stuff? Because you've awakened

> The walk of a
> Master is the
> awakening to
> love of Self.

to your job here. You're part of a group whose journey is to find how to duplicate in physicality what we experience all the time in the nonphysical, because it has never been done en masse, here or anywhere else. We are on the cutting edge of bringing it about. Each one of us who achieves even an above-average love of Self rockets our sleeping species—by that higher frequency—one step closer to the critical mass required to catapult us into the birth of a new era of divine acceleration. And we are very, very close.

So let's get on with it. Let's make this business of learning to love and approve of ourselves—no matter what—our number one priority. The quality of our lives depends on it, our world depends on it, and so does the future of mankind.

We must find cosmic love now, for it is the greatest yearning we have within us. It is also our greatest fear, for it means touching that which we are. Cosmic love is not an emotion, it is the primal force of all Life, the fundamental energy of which we all are made. So we can never "find" love; we can only "be" it. And therein lies the secret. No one is as capable of loving us as we are capable of loving ourselves. We must learn to *flow it out from us* in order to feel it inwardly. Once we find it internally, then we can enhance it with someone else, a partner. But as long as we keep looking outside for that warmth, that tingle of joy, that perceived safety, we will never find the feeling we so desperately seek. As long as we feel unloved to begin with, there's no way we can attract that love. Sex? Yes! Love? No. Pure physics. It just can't happen.

So where do we begin? For openers, we've been loving Self every time we raised our frequency. But to be more specific, here are a few things to remember.

1. Remember that you are worthy of anything you can imagine.

2. When thinking about a regret, find a feeling that feels better.

3. Make a decision to be a lover rather than one wanting to be loved. If you are flowing loving appreciation *to* someone, then you are flooding yourself with that frequency of light, and you will never notice that their river is not currently flowing to you.

(P.S.: As we become filled with our own love, many "special someones" will come into our lives, quite different from what we've assembled in the past!)

4. Make yourself feel "in love" for just a few moments, every day.

5. Whatever you don't want in life, flood it with love (and *vice versa*).

6. Flow this vibration of love out until you're cross-eyed.

7. Make a decision to love *something* about yourself, off and on, all day.

8. Most of all, feel the effervescence of love coming from the pit of your stomach, bubbling up all around you until you can actually feel the tingling, then flow it out from you.

9. Ask for help with learning how to flood yourself with this vibration.

10. Flood everyone with the vibration, *then you become what you flow.* Though it may seem hard to believe, the time will come when it won't matter whether others love you or not, for you have now *become* the love that you sought.

> Love is *not* a two-way street.

HOMEWORK: *Hug-A-Bum*

The energy of love has to be activated, just like Flip-Switching. We may be made of the stuff, but we rarely flow it out of ourselves on any kind of a regular basis or out of habit. So we can create a game to help us practice that magnificent outward flow. The game is called "Hug-A-Bum." No, you won't be running around town hugging every smelly stranger in town. Well, not actually. All we're doing here is learning to activate a flow of love at the drop of a hat, for once we learn what it *feeeeels* like to wrap others in that energy, we can do the same for ourselves, which heals our past, overrides unnecessary old beliefs, pulls in our Desires, and brings in profound peace and joy. *This is **major** Flip-Switching!*

Here's how it works:

> STEP 1: Recall how it feels to have favorite relatives come to your home for the holidays. They arrive at the front door, you open it, and *whoosh*, that feeling of all-encompassing love and joy sweeps over you as you fling your arms around each of them in huge bear hugs, a spontaneous outpouring of pure, unconditional love. Find it! Feel it! *(Fake it, if you have to!)*

> STEP 2: Go where there are people, and pick a "target" (a person) whom you don't know, yet would feel okay having lunch with should the occasion arise. (You'll feel more comfortable and safe that way to start out.)

> STEP 3: In your imagination (which is your God-self in action), see yourself going up to your target to give that big, luscious bear hug just as you did when Aunt Whoosie or Uncle Whatsit came to your front door. See yourself giving your target the biggest bear hug you can muster as that loving joy pours out from you. (Pretend, of course, that your target recognizes you too, and hugs back.)

> STEP 4: Keep doing this—picking targets and seeing yourself run up to hug them as if they were long-lost best friends—until you're comfortable enough to pick a target of a different age or sex or race that you've often felt uncomfortable being around. (In other words, these wouldn't be folks you'd rush to sit next to in a diner.) In consciousness, run up to them and hug them the same way, with totally genuine love, affection, and unabashed joy at seeing them. Do this over and over with these more difficult targets until you can feel the true sincerity of love flowing from you without hesitation. Feel it, and mean it!

> STEP 5: Now comes the biggie. You search out the grungiest, dirtiest, smelliest bum you can find, or bag lady, or drunk in the streets—whatever—and you do the same thing. In consciousness, you surround that being with such unconditional love that the outflow begins to make your head swim. Do it over and over until in

If you want to love you, learn first to flow it from you, then you become what you flow.

consciousness you can genuinely embrace that grand God in the dirty body with a hug that knows no limits with a love that knows no bounds. Remember, all of your targets, bums included, are gods in a body experiencing what they have chosen to express, just as you are doing now.

As you do this, you will often see your targets turn around to see what just happened. They'll never know, but you will. So never, ever "hug" without giving it everything you've got. Never hug without that joy of surprise you experienced at the front door, that elated intoxicating feeling of, "Oh my God, I don't believe it! You're here!"

Hugging a bum or some dude at the supermarket isn't easy. No matter how aware you are that you're just doing this in consciousness, it will probably take some effort and practice before you can toss caution to the wind, pretend to wrap your arms around the dirtiest thing on two feet, and truly love them. Once you can do that, and feel it and mean it, you'll know you've changed.

Now Listen Up

Who you are internally is the most loved and beautiful thing the universe has ever created. None of you were accidents. You were all intentional creations, loved beyond your comprehension into existence. Maybe your parents didn't want you, but from a universal standpoint, each of you was a "planned pregnancy."

The universe has no standards for us. It will never withhold love. Not ever! No matter what we do, have done, or will do, the universe will never, ever withhold its love. We could be the most criminally insane people on this planet, and the love would never be withheld. I beg you to feel the truth of those words.

This is the last leg of our journey to self-realization. And it is the hardest, because we must learn to be unconditional in our love of Self; because we must let go, once and for all, of our games of unworthiness; and because we must learn to feel what supports us, rather than continue to live with the erroneous belief that we are any "less than" that from which we were birthed. Our eternal need for approval is only a mask to keep us from our own love.

Do you want to get over being timid? Then learn to love your timidity. Want to get over needing attention or approval or love? Then learn to love what you want to put behind you. Turning on to flood our bodies with whatever we want to change removes our focus from what we no longer want about us. The reason we're not happy with some part of ourselves is because we're not letting Source energy into it, meaning love.

> Unworthiness was a lesson; now love it into wisdom.

We don't need to hang on to these outmoded guilts or shames or inadequacies any longer. What we need to do is stand up, brush ourselves off, and start acting and feeling like the Gods we are. We need to stomp our Godfoot and say to all of our masks and excuses that are keeping us from touching our Source energy, "Get outta here! I'm done with you," as we Flip-Switch into appreciation for what they have given us, and then flood them with love.

When you're flowing high, you're feeling great. And when you're bombarding someone (or something) with love or appreciation or marvel or awe or respect or gratitude, you are not berating yourself. Disapproval comes only from the past, and high, pure, positive energy flows only in the Divine Now.

As with Hug-A-Bum, if you will force yourself to flow love and appreciation toward another, no matter what that other represents to *you—no matter what—you* will automatically begin to find acceptance within yourself. It cannot be otherwise, because the high vibration of love overrides the low vibration of self-denigration.

Love of one's self must be unconditional. If you continue to put up roadblocks such as "I'll love myself *only* when I stop doing blah-blah," you're automatically including that roadblock in your vibration—to grow and cause trouble. But you don't have to change your old beliefs about how insecure you are or how sinful or how dorky. You just have to find a thought that makes you feel better. And another, and another, until the habit of new thought replaces the old.

You are a creator, an extension of Source energy. Your power is unlimited, but that power must be exercised to create. It must be exercised to walk you out of self-doubt. It must be exercised for you to Flip-Switch from something that doesn't feel good to something that feels a whole lot better. If it doesn't feel good when you think about it, it's not *good for* you! Change it!

Approving of ourselves can become really easy if we just remember that our only job is to search around for thoughts that make us feel better until both the feelings and the thoughts become a habit pattern. The more we practice searching for better feelings, the sooner our reality shifts to match those new vibrations.

So become a lover of self and others, rather than a seeker of love. Become an approver of every dumb thing you do/did, say/said, or think/thought. Not that you'd repeat it, but you can still approve of it for the lesson. Give generously to yourself until you can feel the joy of that giving, rather than the guilt. Script the end results you desire, and the universe will create miracles all around you. Find the appropriate feeling, and make that decision to approve of yourself, *no matter what*. In all eternity, you have not one reason not to.

To approve of one's self
is to know divine love.

Finding your God

Quietly center yourself into that special place that you most enjoy. Let the high-vibrational sprinkles of violet sparks fall all over and about you. Ask all who walk with you to participate in this meditation with you. Then ask your Inner Being—the You of you—to come to the forefront to be felt and known.

Begin to repeat to yourself, "I am love, I am love, I am love," bringing up the feelings to a level of passion. Keep repeating this to yourself or out loud until your heart and being swell with emotion. No longer allow yourself to fear this love, for it is the divine energy we must touch to become whole.

If tears come, let them. Stay focused, repeating, "I am love, I am love," and *feeeeeling* whatever you feel. Make yourself feel it, that God that you are within.

Begin to notice, now, any excuses that come up, any resistance, pain or struggle, or even longing for more or not knowing what to do with the intensity. Go deeper, and *feeeeel*. Search, find, and feel!

Within your being there is a God, and it is time to find it. So push to the deepest part of your being as you repeat, "I am love, I am love." Perhaps what you feel will be a warmth or a tenderness or even a joy. Perhaps you will feel a true love. Whatever you feel, let it come.

And now, from this place of security, push out the struggle. Just push it out of you! Push out the loneliness, the pain, the old beliefs, and exchange them for the love that holds you. Ask your guides for help in this as you literally push out from your body all remaining limited thinking, whether you are still aware of it or not. As all of this leaves you, see it being drenched in the violet sparkles dancing about you.

> **INSIGHT**
> When you have loved the hurt not to matter, you are complete.

For one last time, go deeper into that space of love. And now say to yourself, and feel, "I am loved, I am loved, I am loved." Feel clean, feel washed in your own pure vibration. Thank your guides, thank the God you are, and come ever so slowly back to a very new You.

About the Author

Lynn Grabhorn began her spiritual journey in the '80s, but soon found that most spiritual books were written in such a high, "grand" tone, they were less than appealing to read. So she decided that if these so-called great masters couldn't bring themselves down to the human level of thinking and understanding, she'd do it herself. The rather kicky, somewhat irreverent manner in which she wrote *Excuse Me, Your Life Is Waiting* has made such a hit, the book has become a best-seller around the world, and Lynn has brought that same upbeat fun into the *Excuse Me... Playbook*.

Other Books by Lynn Grabhorn
Beyond the Twelve Steps
Excuse Me, Your Life Is Waiting
Dear God! What's Happening to Us?
Planet Two

Hampton Roads Publishing Company

... for the evolving human spirit

Hampton Roads Publishing Company
publishes books on a variety of subjects,
including spirituality, health, and other
related topics.

For a copy of our latest trade catalog,
call 978-465-0504 or visit our website at *www.hrpub.com*